Religion
In Radical Transition

Religion
In Radical Transition

Edited by

JEFFREY K. HADDEN

ta
Transaction Books
New Brunswick, New Jersey
Distributed by E.P. Dutton & Co., Inc.

Transaction Books
Rutgers University
New Brunswick, New Jersey 08903

Library of Congress Catalog Number: 74-133305
ISBN: 0-87855-070-4 (cloth); 0-87855-567-6 (paper)

Printed in the United States of America

Contents

Preface

For the past decade, *trans*action, and now **Society**, has dedicated itself to the task of reporting the strains and conflicts within the American system. But the magazine has done more than this. It has pioneered in social programs for changing the social order, offered the kind of analysis that has permanently restructured the terms of the "dialogue" between peoples and publics, and offered the sort of prognosis that makes for real alterations in economic and political policies directly affecting our lives.

The work done in the magazine has crossed disciplinary boundaries. This represents much more than simple cross-disciplinary "team efforts." It embodies rather a recognition that the social world cannot be easily carved into neat academic disciplines; that, indeed, the study of the experience of blacks in American ghettos, or the manifold uses and abuses of agencies of law enforcement, or the sorts of overseas policies that lead to the celebration of some dictatorships and the condemnation of others, can best be examined from many viewpoints and from the vantage points of many disciplines.

The editors of **Society** magazine are now making available in permanent form the most important work done in the magazine, supplemented in some cases by additional materials edited to reflect the tone and style developed over the years by *trans*action. Like the magazine, this series of books demonstrates the superiority of starting with real world problems and searching out practical solutions, over the zealous guardianship of professional boundaries. Indeed, it is precisely this approach that has elicited enthusiastic support from leading American social scientists, many of whom are represented among the editors of these volumes.

The subject matter of these books concerns social changes and social policies that have aroused the long-standing needs and present-day anxieties of us all. These changes are in organizational lifestyles, concepts of human ability and intelligence, changing patterns of norms and morals, the relationship of social conditions to physical and biological environments, and in the status of social science with respect to national policy making. The editors feel that many of these articles have withstood the test of time, and match in durable interest the best of available social science literature. This collection of essays, then, attempts to address itself to immediate issues without violating the basic insights derived from the classical literature in the various fields of social science.

As the political crises of the sixties have given way to the economic crunch of the seventies, the social scientists involved as editors and authors of this series have gone beyond observation of critical areas, and have entered into the vital and difficult tasks of explanation and interpretation. They have defined issues in a way that makes solutions possible. They have provided answers as well as asked the right questions. These books, based as they are upon the best materials from *trans*action/**Society** magazine, are dedicated to highlighting social problems alone, and beyond that, to establishing guidelines for social solutions based on the social sciences.

The remarkable success of the book series to date is indicative of the need for such "fastbacks" in college course work and, no less, in the everyday needs of busy people who have not surrendered the need to know, nor the lively sense required to satisfy such knowledge needs. It is also plain that what superficially appeared as a random selection of articles on the basis of subject alone, in fact, represented a careful concern for materials that are addressed to issues at the shank and marrow of society. It is the distillation of the best of these, systematically arranged, that appears in these volumes.

THE EDITORS
*trans*action/**Society**

Introduction

JEFFREY K. HADDEN

During the first eight years of the publication of *trans-action*, 15 articles have been devoted to religion. All dealt either directly or indirectly with conflict and turmoil within religious institutions or religious belief systems. Given the orientation of the editors (see the preface to this volume) one might legitimately question whether this represents a balanced perspective on the status of religion in contemporary society.

I believe that it does, for religion is in a period of radical change and upheaval—more so than at any point since the Protestant Reformation. It makes no sense to speak of ecumenism in the United States, the plethora of religious cults in Asia, or the religious implications of drug use among youth and the avant garde unless one recognizes these developments as manifestations of the failure of traditional religious institutions and belief systems to provide meaning in these terribly complicated times. One cannot intelligently address the issue of religion as a scholar, as a practicioner, or even as an informal conversationalist unless one first comes to grips with this fact.

It is perhaps too early to know whether religious institutions are about to go out of business or if they are in the midst of internal struggles that will lead them not only to adapt but also to become dynamic and viable sources of leadership and direction amid social upheaval. My own informed judgment at this point sees the institutions coming to their end of the line. The only real issue seems to be whether they will experience a rapid and violent death or if the process will be a slow, silent demise reflecting the institutions' irrelevance to the human community.

From my vantage point the churches have long lost their relevance to much of what is happening, although, to be sure, this is not so to the millions who profess and practice their faith. Still, shrinking church attendance and mounting financial difficulties seem to suggest significant growth in the number of churchgoers who have something less than unquestioning allegiance to the institution, if not the faith. My bone of contention with the institutions lies in their having permitted the churches to serve as escapes from the world. This, of course, is also the bone of contention of many within the churches, especially the new breed of clergy, who seek to shock the institutions from their complacency to face the realities created by the staggering revolutions of technology and population growth.

I seriously doubt whether the reformers within the churches have the authority, the influence, or the political sophistication to alter the organizational structures or the values of the membership to a degree that will make any significant difference. In their efforts to do so in this country, they have brought to the surface all of the latent conflict that has been simmering for decades.

In my book, *The Gathering Storm in the Churches*, I attempted to describe and interpret the central developments emerging in contemporary religious institutions around three deeply intertwined crises of doctrinal belief, the meaning and purpose of the church and the exercise of authority. The data that were amassed, both my own and what I used of other scholars' work to argue the validity of the thesis, were probably the most extensive ever assembled in a social science inquiry of religion. The response of many well informed churchmen to my work consisted in "so what's new?" or "why go to such pains to document the obvious?" Social scientists have always felt a bit on the defensive about this type of criticism of their labors and we have all probably developed a repertoire of examples of findings that turn out to be just the opposite of broadly held folk beliefs.

At the heart of the issue, however, is the incredible degree to which our position in the social structure shapes our construction of reality. To the churchman caught up in these struggles, my arguments ring true, if somewhat trivial. But many of them fail to understand the extent to which other churchgoers interpret the thesis in quite different terms and see very different implications, while still others see the thesis as quite irrelevant to anything happening in religion in our society.

The students at the National Democratic Convention in Chicago who faced the charging police and shouted "the whole world is watching," as the television cameras rolled, failed to understand that the large majority of American society witnessed something quite different, and did so in spite of the television commentators' sympathetic treatment of the students' interpretation of reality. Public opinion polls made it quite clear that the large majority of American society considered the police and Mayor Daley quite justified in their behavior.

In discussing the educational imperitives of our society, Kenneth Boulding put the case quite eloquently when he wrote "[we need] to develop a lively appreciation of the nature and necessity of sampling and a distrust of purely personal experience." If the social scientists' data collection move us beyond personal experience to see the world as others see it, then it seems to me that our labors are quite justified and worth the effort.

Unfortunately, the discovery of broader conceptions of reality is only the first step in the development of wisdom. The more difficult task remains: interpreting the new knowledge and understanding its implications. To take this task seriously is to go full circle and be forced to rely on our personal experience, for the data have themselves become a part of our personal experience and our understanding of reality.

To develop an appreciation of the value of social science, it is necessary to understand that there are few issues where the data are all in and the final word can be written. This is especially true with the topic of religion, for, until about a decade ago, we had almost no data at all. While the sixties witnessed the amassing of a great deal of empirical data on religion, those of us working in the field are painfully aware of how much knowledge we lack. When one attempts to speculate about the implications of the data, one must face the agonizing reality that perhaps there are developments going on "out there" that we haven't adequately investigated and therefore do not understand, and if we did, perhaps we would see the implications of present knowledge in quite a different light.

I am quite sympathetic with those who criticize the social scientists for standing aloof from their data. Too often we have hidden behind slogans like "value-free" and "objective," refusing to speculate about the implications of data unmistakably loaded with social meaning. One of the consequences of the tumultuous sixties has been a growing awareness among social scientists that we can't have our cake and eat it too. If we believe that systematic knowledge is superior to ignorance, superstition and tradition, then we have to accept responsibility for the implications of our knowledge.

Still, the very process and discipline whereby one learns to ask systematic empirical questions leads one to have an appreciation of the tenuous and precarious nature of social data. It is one thing to examine the data and to feel personally that one understands their implications. It is quite another thing to assume responsibility for these conclusions in the public marketplace. The broader the meaning a set of findings has for the basic fabric of society, the more difficult it becomes to speak up with conviction.

To state that the churches are about to go out of business is a serious proposition, particularly if one has an appreciation of the important historical role they have played in defining, sustaining and transmitting human values and integrating society. If the present forms of institutionalized religion are on their way out, the serious student of society must ask what institutions or systems of values and meaning can replace them. Is it possible for a pluralistic society questioning almost every aspect of traditional values to survive without any overarching system of meaning—save a vague and nebulously defined humanism? Obviously no one can answer this question. It does seem clear, however, that the wisdom of the most "advanced" societies has only succeeded in creating more devastating mechanisms for man to perpetrate inhumane acts on his fellow man. And this realization forces a sobering perspective on the easy assumption that education and rationality can create a humanitarianism capable of replacing the traditional functions of institutionalized religion.

I am not assuming that religion has always been on the side of humanitarianism. Indeed, the evidence is quite clear that it has not. I am simply trying to place the issue of the demise of religion in the context of history. Our understanding of the role of religion in history is quite inadequate. In the absence of a more adequate history, we ought not to take the demise of religion lightly, for there seems to be considerable evidence that religion has not only supported the status quo but has also on occasions provided solid legitimacy to movements of change and humanitarianism.

In admitting the precarious nature of social science data, I must also acknowledge the possibility that I may be misreading the evidence on the future of religion. Perhaps the questions I raise are tainted by my own narrow experience and are not really very important, or perhaps they are focused on the wrong issues. However, I think that the careful reader of this volume will see some of the intellectual roots of my concern.

The articles published in *trans*action do not contain all the significant developments in religion during the past decade. What surprised me in assembling the materials for this volume is that the editors have captured so much. The issues they have missed are largely missing in the social science literature. Perhaps the most serious is some provocative theoretical developments in the sociology of religion. The most important theoretical synthesis, in my judgment, is Peter Berger's volume, *The Sacred Canopy*. I shall review its central arguments here because I believe it will add substance to the comments I have made thus far as well as provide an important perspective for interpreting several of the articles in this volume.

Berger's central argument is that the demise of religion was built into the very structure and foundations of the Judeo-Christian tradition. Building on the theoretical perspective developed in his earlier work, *The Social Construction of Reality* (co-authored with Thomas Luckmann), he sees human society as a world-building enterprise involving a dialectical process by which man both creates and is a product of society. Objective and subjective values, which are taken for granted, give meaning to and legitimate social reality. But the meaningful order that man gives to human experience is, for a variety of reasons, inherently unstable. Man is able to resolve this inherent precariousness by moving outside of himself and establishing a sacred cosmos—an external legitimating force which will explain and justify the social order. In short, religion is able to "locate" human experience within a sacred cosmic frame of reference capable of imposing order and meaning on the ever-present threat of chaos.

But religion itself is also inherently precarious since it is the product of human experience and grows out of man's understanding of the plausible. Since man's understanding of the plausible can be altered by the experience of history, religious presuppositions are subject to change and reinterpretation. Some changes or reinterpretations may fall within the parameters of the plausibility structures, but others may set in motion change that will undercut the plausibility of a religious faith. This is precisely what is happening to Christianity and quite probably all the important world religions.

The Christian faith has been experiencing a serious devaluation of the plausibility of its basic legitimizing tenents. Secularization—the removal of society from the domination of religious symbols and institutions—has its origins in the Old Testament, but several historical developments have intensified the process. The rise of Protestantism was especially critical for it divested the Christian faith of three of its most powerful concomitants of cosmic legitimacy: mystery, miracle, and magic.

At the same time, a rapidly changing economic-industrial order caused significant strains on established social structures. The declining plausibility of the established religious order weakened its position to legitimize the traditional social order, which in turn paved the way for an accelerated pace of change in other orders.

Today man is confronted with a "crisis of credibility" in religion. He lives in a world of many religions as well as other "reality-defining agencies," none of which has the power to impose its conception of reality on the world and demand man's allegiance. Religion has passed from the responsibility of the state to numerous voluntary associations which must compete in a marketplace for loyalty and adherence to doctrine. Ecumenicity is viewed by Berger as a cartelization; the number of competing institutions is reduced and the market is organized by mutual agreements.

What, then, is the future of religious institutions and how will the historic role of providing cosmic legitimacy to man's social reality be achieved? Berger at least implies an answer to the first question as follows: ". . .'reality' becomes a 'private' affair of individuals, that is, loses the quality of self-evident intersubjective plausibility—thus one 'cannot really talk' about religion any more. . .religion no longer refers to the cosmos or to history, but to individual *Existenz* or psychology."

Unfortunately, Berger leaves the second question virtually unexplored. But the question is too important to be left to theologians and philosophers. What is at stake is more than the demise or radical reorganization of a major social institution. If Berger is correct, we are experiencing a restructuring of meaning which is at least as profound in its implications as the technological-industrial revolution and the population explosion. Modern man may not be so much estranged or alienated from meaning as he is alone and without meaning outside the self. New Frontiers, a Great Society or a world where men can live in peace with justice may tantalize the imagination, but the obstacles to their attainment appear overwhelming.

These thoughts are not original. Perhaps what is important is that social scientists, employing different methods and beginning with different assumptions, have arrived at an important crossroad with other disciplines.

It would be easy for well-meaning, overly enthusiastic social scientists, dedicated to a favorable solution of the dilemmas faced by homo sapiens on this tiny planet, to rush forth and assume a self-proclaimed Godlike role. It would be perhaps even easier for others to relinquish their responsibility as policy makers to these zealous social scientists. The only catch, as Irving Louis Horowitz has pointed out, is "If the sociologist [social scientist] at all times had a set of values, knowledge, and wisdom superior to those he is dedicated to study, there would be no problem. The rub is that the hardest thing to establish is a claim to superiority." Perhaps the lesson of the sixties, a decade which more than any previous one, pressured social scientists to engage in policy research, lies in an appreciation of the precariousness of the social science enterprise—both as collector and systematizer of data and as consultant and policy maker. This is not to say that social scientists should disengage themselves from the world; the unfolding of history does not really leave us this choice. We must, however, attempt to understand the limitations of our data and communicate with those who would utilize our findings in public policy.

These moral ambiguities rise to the surface in attempting to speculate on the implications of the findings in this volume. As indicated at the beginning, the theories and empirical findings of the social sciences suggest a doubtful future for religious institutions. The conflict and internal tensions within Protestantism and Catholicism seem quite inescapable. Holding onto traditional beliefs and practices involves a gradual but certain estrangement from the critical problems of our society. Religious groups that cling to the "old time religion" seem to be buying time against the inevitable forces of history—though obviously most of them do not see it this way. While providing a comfort and escape for their members, they are more and more becoming a part of the problem by enhancing alienation from society.

Those groups who demythologize and attempt to "make religion relevant" to the modern world are facing a different set of problems. They are discovering tremendous resistance to efforts aimed at enacting policies consistent with their understanding of the implications of Christian teachings in matters of brotherhood and social justice. They are also discovering that decline in orthodoxy results in a general decline in all forms of religious commitment.

Few are particularly enthusiastic about facing these and other conclusions dropped on their doorstep by social scientists. Some religionists dismiss social science as a meaningful way to gain insight into the nature and consequences of religious belief and practice. Others challenge the validity of any finding that is not "favorable" to religion. Some have even engaged their own researchers, most with dubious qualifications, to "prove" that the findings of Charles Glock and Rodney Stark are wrong. This is very much like the tobacco industry employing its own researchers to "prove" smoking does not cause cancer. Still others have accepted the findings of social science quite uncritically and used them in ways that are quite questionable, to support political battles within the churches.

Perhaps there is hope in the realization that someone is paying attention to our work, even if much of the attention is negative. None of the social science studies of religion is invulnerable to methodological criticism and the need for further refinement. Yet, we are reluctant to say this too loudly lest we give those not favorably disposed toward social science cause to dismiss us without serious thought.

Our work has raised many more questions than it has satisfactorily answered, and we are anxious to get on with exploring these issues. However, the structural matrix within which we operate seems destined to make this a difficult task in the years ahead.

The government and the big foundations are reluctant to fund studies of religion; the former hiding behind the shield of separation of church and state and the latter behind the "charter of the foundation" or a "different set of priorities for funding this year." Only the churches have money to study religion. If they would pool their resources and engage competent researchers, they could learn a great deal that would be helpful to them in better understanding the present and in planning for the future. But to accomplish this would probably be more difficult than reorganizing the structure of metropolitan government in America. Even where money is available, tremendous internal pressures are present to engage researchers who are members of the faith, while competence as a social scientist seems to be of the lowest priority. The results may legitimize the programs and whims of church administrators, but they seldom add to our understanding of the nature and consequences of religious belief or the structure and functioning of religious institutions.

The monies that permitted significant development in our knowledge of religion during the past decade were in part windfalls and in part involved the courageous "misuse" of funds. No substantial source of funding appears forthcoming in the immediate future. Some social scientists interested in religion will solve this problem of support by moving to other areas of interest. Others may resolve the dilemma by becoming "sympathetic" insiders, but they run a high risk of spreading their talents thin and producing more descriptive studies with low levels of theoretical and empirical generalizability.

All of this would seem to suggest that the scientific study of religion, like religious institutions themselves, faces a bleak and uncertain future. If *trans*action repeats this series of books in another five or ten years, religion could well be absent because of lack of progress in the scientific exploration of the field. It will not be omitted because religious institutions have ceased to experience the tugs and strains of radical transition.

If there is some basis for a more optimistic prognosis for the future systematic study of religion, it seems to me that it grows out of the prospect of a radical shift of emphasis in the direction of inquiry. With the secularization of society, religion is no longer the only institution providing meaning and legitimacy to the social order. To be sure, if we take Berger's arguments in *The Sacred Canopy* seriously, this is at the heart of man's contemporary crisis of meaning and authority. But Berger's work, as well as Richard L. Mean's provocative commentary in his recent book, *The Ethical Imperative*, have broader implications for the direction and emphasis in sociological inquiry. Both point to the need to understand more clearly the nature, sources and sustenance of human values.

Perhaps those of us who have criticized the parochialism of "religious sociologists" have ourselves been guilty of defining the scope of our inquiry too narrowly. Perhaps our critical point of departure ought not to be religion but rather the study of values. Several critical shifts of emphasis occur from this perspective. First, by placing religion in the broader context of the study of values, it becomes more apparent that the literature here is also sparse. Sociologists and psychologists have developed literally hundreds of instruments to measure various attitudinal concepts or "dimensions," but the more fundamental task of understanding the nature, sources and structure of human values has received much less attention. There is a need for both theoretical and empirical breakthrough at this level.

Such a shift in emphasis also indicates the need to devote greater attention to values in a cross-cultural perspective. Most of the research in the sociology of religion during the past decade has been terribly ethnocentric. The very fact that most of the research instruments do not seem applicable to non-Western socioreligious cultures should suggest the potential theoretical payoff of broader cross-cultural perspectives.

The potential rewards of a shift in emphasis could be developed at some length, but perhaps the most critical point is that such a shift would bring us closer to the critical problems of a society and world in turmoil. We are beginning to understand a great deal about the nature of the problems created by the world's exploding population, the unleashing of energy and scientific-technological development, the exploitation of natural resources, etc. Scientists and politicians alike are coming around to the view that solutions to our many problems are not technological but social. It is increasingly difficult to hear or read anyone addressing themselves to the issue of social change without encountering references to a need to "reorder our priorities," "rethink our values," etc. But this is an extremely difficult thing to do when, in fact, our scientific understanding of the nature and structure of values is very crude. We have long made conceptual distinctions between attitudes and values, but in our research the distinction is much fuzzier. Perhaps we have identified some underlying value dimensions, but even this is not at all clear. And how can we change that which we do not understand?

This shift of emphasis which I propose does not negate the importance of studying religion. In fact, it broadens the scope of questions we ought to be asking about religion. What is the historical role of religious values, authority and institutions? How are these changing and why? What are the possibilities and limitations of religion as a source of social change, as an inhibitor of change and as an integrating force in human society? How do religious values fit into the broader matrix of emerging and changing human values? Adequate answers to these questions take us well beyond the present empirical and theoretical insights of the sociology and psychology of religion. This is not to suggest the futility of the developments in the scientific study of religion during the past decade. To the contrary, it is these developments which now permit us to refocus our thinking about the future of religion.

I: BELIEF AND PRACTICE IN CONFLICT

Paradoxes of Religious Belief

MILTON ROKEACH

All organized western religious groups teach their adherents, and those they try to convert, contradictory sets of beliefs. On the one hand, they teach mutual love and respect, the golden rule, the love of justice and mercy, and to regard all men as equal in the eyes of God. On the other hand, they teach (implicitly if not openly) that only certain people can be saved—those who believe as they do; that only certain people are chosen people; that there is only one real truth—theirs.

Throughout history man, inspired by religious motives, has indeed espoused noble and humanitarian ideals and often behaved accordingly. But he has also committed some of the most horrible crimes and wars in the holy name of religion—the massacre of St. Bartholomew, the Crusades, the Inquisitions, the pogroms and the burnings of witches and heretics.

This is the fundamental paradox of religious belief. It is not confined to history. In milder but even more personal forms it exists in our daily lives.

In 1949 Clifford Kirkpatrick, professor of sociology at Indiana University, published some findings on the relationship between religious sentiments and humanitarian attitudes. Professor Kirkpatrick investigated the oft-heard contention that religious feeling fosters humanitarianism; and, conversely that those without religious training should therefore be less humanitarian. His conclusions were surprising—at least to the followers of organized religion. In group after group—Catholic, Jewish and the Protestant denominations—he found little correlation at all; but what there was was negative. That is, the devout tended to be slightly less humanitarian and had more punitive attitudes toward criminals, delinquents, prostitutes, homosexuals and those who might seem in need of psychological counseling or psychiatric treatment.

In my own research I have found that, on the average, those who identify themselves as belonging to a religious organization express more intolerance toward racial and ethnic groups (other than their own) than do non-believers —or even Communists. These results have been found at Michigan State University, at several New York colleges, and in England (where the Communist results were obtained). Gordon Allport in his book, *The Nature of Prejudice*, describes many of the studies that have come up with similar findings. In a recent paper he read at the Crane Theological School of Tufts University, he said:

> On the average, church goers and professedly religious people have considerably more prejudice than do non-church goers and non-believers.

Actually, this conclusion is not quite accurate. While nonbelievers are in fact generally less prejudiced than believers toward racial and ethnic groups, it does not follow that they are more tolerant in every respect. Nonbelievers often betray a bigotry and intellectual arrogance of another kind—intolerance toward those who disagree with them. Allport's conclusion is valid if by "prejudice" we only mean ethnic and religious prejudice.

Organized religion also contends that the religious have greater "peace of mind" and mental balance. We have found in our research at Michigan State University— described in my book, *The Open and Closed Mind*—that people with formal religious affiliation are more anxious. Believers, compared with nonbelievers, complain more often of working under great tension, sleeping fitfully and similar symptoms. On a test designed to measure manifest anxiety, believers generally scored higher than non-believers.

If religious affiliation and anxiety go together, is there also a relation between religion and serious mental disturbance? What is the relative frequency of believers and nonbelievers in mental hospitals, compared to the outside? Are the forms and courses of their illnesses different? I recently discussed this with the clinical director of a large mental hospital. He believes without question that religious sentiments prevail in a majority of his patients; further, that religious delusions play a major part in the illnesses of about a third of them.

It is pretty hard to conclude from such observations anything definite about the role religion plays in mental health. This is an area that needs much research, not only within our own culture but also cross-culturally. I am thinking especially of the Soviet Union. What is the relative frequency of mental disease in the Soviet Union as compared with western countries? To what extent could such differences be attributable to differences in religious sentiments? What is the proportion of believers and non-believers in Soviet mental hospitals? Many questions could be asked.

In a study in Lansing, Michigan, we found that when

you ask a group of Catholics to rank the major Christian denominations in order of their similarity to Catholicism, you generally get the following order: Catholic first, then Episcopalian, Lutheran, Presbyterian, Methodist and finally Baptist. Ask a group of Baptists to rank the same denominations for similarity, and you get exactly the reverse order: Baptist, Methodist, Presbyterian, Lutheran, Episcopalian and finally Catholic. When we look at the listings of similarities they seem to make up a kind of color wheel, with each one of the six major Christian groups judging all other positions from its own standpoint along the continuum. But actually it turns out that all these continua are basically variations of the same theme, with Catholics at one end and Baptists at the other.

Apparently people build up mental maps of which religions are similar to their own, and these mental maps have an important influence on everyday behavior. If a Catholic decides to leave his church and join another, the probability is greatest that he will join the Episcopalian church—next the Lutheran church—and so on down the line. Conversely, a defecting Baptist will more probably join the Methodist church, after that the Presbyterian church, and so on. The other denominations follow the same pattern.

The probability of interfaith marriage increases with the similarity between denominations. When a Catholic marries someone outside his faith, it is more likely to be an Episcopalian, next most likely a Lutheran, and so on.

What of the relation between marital conflicts and interfaith marriages? In general we find that the greater the dissimilarity, the greater likelihood of conflict both before and after marriage.

We determined this by restricting our analysis to couples of whom at least one partner was always Methodist. We interviewed seven or eight all Methodist couples; then another group in which Methodists had married Presbyterians; then Methodists and Lutherans; and on around. We not only questioned them about their marital conflicts, but also about their pre-marital conflicts. How long did they "go steady"? (The assumption is that the longer you go steady beyond a certain point, the more likely the conflict.) Did parents object to the marriage? Had they themselves had doubts about it beforehand? Had they ever broken off their engagement? For marital conflict, we asked questions about how often they quarreled, whether they had ever separated (if so, how many times), and whether they had ever contemplated divorce. From the answers we constructed an index of premarital and postmarital conflict.

These findings raise an issue of interest to us all. From the standpoint of mental health, it can be argued that interfaith marriages are undesirable. From the standpoint of democracy, is it desirable to have a society in which everyone marries only within his own sect or denomination? This is a complicated matter and cannot be pursued here. But these findings do suggest that somehow the average person has gotten the idea that religious differences—even minor denominational distinctions within the Christian fold—do make a difference; so much difference in fact that interfaith marriages must result in mental unhappiness.

To pull together the various findings: I have mentioned that empirical results show that religious people are on the average less humanitarian, more bigoted, more anxious; also that the greater the religious differences, the greater the likelihood of conflict in marriage. Does a common thread run through these diverse results? What lessons can we learn from them?

It seems to me that these results cannot be accounted for by assuming, as the antireligionists do, that religion is an unqualified force for evil; nor by assuming, as the pro-religionists do, that religion is a force only for good. Instead, as indicated at the beginning, I believe that these results become more understandable if we assume that there exist simultaneously, within the organized religions of the West, psychologically conflicting moral forces for good and evil—teaching brotherhood with the right hand and bigotry with left, facilitating mental health in some and mental conflict, anxiety and psychosis in others. I realize that this seems an extreme interpretation; but the research bears it out. Gordon Allport makes a similar point:

> Brotherhood and bigotry are intertwined in all religion. Plenty of pious persons are saturated with racial, ethnic, and other prejudice. But at the same time many of the most ardent advocates of racial justice are religiously motivated.

We are taught to make definite distinctions between "we" and "they," between believer and nonbeliever; and sometimes we are urged to act on the basis of these distinctions, for instance in marriage. The category of man that comes to mind when we hear the word "infidel" or "heretic" is essentially a religious one. It is part of our religious heritage. But it is pretty difficult psychologically to love infidels and heretics to the same extent that we love believers. The psychological strain must be very great; and a major result must be guilt and anxiety.

This kind of dichotomy is not confined to religion. Gunnar Myrdal, in *The American Dilemma,* described the conflict between American ideals of democracy and practice of discrimination against minority groups, and the guilt, anxiety and disorder it spawned. We are familiar in international affairs with the enormous psychological discrepancy between the humanitarian ideals of a classless society advocated by the Marxists and the antihumanitarian methods employed by them for its achievement. No wonder there have been so many defections from the Communist cause in America and Europe! When the strain between one set of beliefs and another set of beliefs—or between belief and practice—becomes too great, one natural response is to turn away from the whole system.

I suspect that such contradictions lead often to defection from religion also. Most of the time, however, the result is psychological conflict, anxiety and chronic discomfort arising from feelings of guilt. The contradictions in religious teachings are more subtle than those in politics and would, for the most part, be denied consciously. A conflict between ideological content and ideological structure—between what is taught and how it is taught—must be very subtle. A particular religious institution not only must disseminate a particular religious ideology; it must also perpetuate itself and defend against outside attack. It is this dual purpose of religious institutions, I hypothesize, which leads to the contradiction between the what and the how. It leads to the paradox of a church disseminating truly religious values to the extent possible, while unwittingly communicating antireligious values to the extent necessary.

Gordon Allport, writing on the relation between religion and bigotry, has suggested two types of religious orientation. He calls them the extrinsic and the intrinsic. The extrinsic outlook on religion is utilitarian, self-centered, opportunistic and other-directed. The intrinsic, in contrast, includes basic trust, a compassionate understanding of others so that "dogma is tempered with humility" and, with increasing maturity, "is no longer limited to single segments of self interest." Allport does not imply that everyone is purely either intrinsic or extrinsic; rather, all range somewhere along the continuum from one pole to the other.

The extent to which a particular person has an intrinsic or extrinsic outlook depends largely on the way he is able to resolve the contradictory teachings of his religious group.

This in turn depends on the particular quality of his experiences with others, especially with parents in early childhood. A person is more apt to be extrinsically-oriented if his early experiences included threat, anxiety and punishment or if religion was used punitively, as a club to discipline and control him.

Good empirical evidence exists which supports Allport's distinctions. W. Cody Wilson has succeeded in isolating and measuring the extrinsic religious sentiment and in showing that it is closely related to anti-Semitism. Also, one of my collaborators, Dr. G. Gratton Kemp, has isolated two kinds of religiously-minded students, all enrolled in one denominational college. One group was open-minded and tolerant. The other group was closed-minded and highly prejudiced. Dr. Kemp studied their value orientations over a six-year period. He found that while they expressed similar values when in college, they diverged sharply six years later. Both groups ranked their religious values highest but then parted abruptly. The open-minded group put social values next and theoretical values third. The closed-minded group also ranked religious values highest, but political values were second in importance for them and economic values third. It is obvious that the total cluster of values is quite different between the open-minded and the closed-minded groups. These findings clearly suggest that religious people do indeed differ strongly in their orientations toward life to the extent that their religious outlook is, as Allport claims, extrinsic or intrinsic.

All the preceding leads to the following tentative conclusions: the fact that religious people are more likely to express antihumanitarian attitudes, bigotry and anxiety and the fact that religious similarity and dissimilarity play an important role in marital conflict may both be interpreted as the end result of the emergence of the extrinsic rather than the intrinsic orientation toward religion. They also suggest that, in most people, the extrinsic orientation predominates. This greater prominence of extrinsic attitudes in turn seems to arise out of the contradictory beliefs transmitted through organized religion: humanitarian on one side, antihumanitarian on the other. One constructive suggestion that might be advanced is that ministers, rabbis, and priests should better understand the differences between the what and the how of belief, and the fact that contradictions between the what and the how can lead to excessive anxiety, pervasive guilt, and psychic conflict and, therefore, to all sorts of defensive behavior capable of alleviating guilt and conflict. Representatives of organized religion should consequently become more sophisticated about the unwitting contradictions introduced into religious teachings, and try to eliminate them—as the Catholics are doing now with belief in Jewish guilt for the crucifixion.

Parents are really the middlemen between the forces of organized religion and the child. What factors in rearing, in parental attitudes, in discipline techniques, in the quality or reward and punishment are likely to lead to what Allport has called the intrinsic orientation toward religion? What factors lead to the extrinsic? The data suggest that the more the parent encourages the formation and development of extrinsic attitudes toward religion, the more he hinders the growth of the child into a mature and healthy human being. The more he strengthens the intrinsic religious orientation, the more he helps his child grow healthy, mature, tolerant, and happy.

The conflict between the ideal and what seems to be the practical is widespread. But the current readjustment in racial relations, in which clergymen have taken so large a part, for all its upset and pain indicates that these dichotomies are neither eternal nor inevitable. Nor is the extrinsic orientation necessarily the "practical" one. Research and practice in race relations, criminology and child-rearing have consistently shown that the nonpunitive and accepting approach brings better results.

Change is underway, in the church and in the home, and brings with it, hopefully, greater emphasis on resolving the paradox between the what and the how of religious belief.

January/February 1965

Is There an American Protestantism?

CHARLES Y. GLOCK/RODNEY STARK

"Do you, personally, believe in God?" To this recurrent question on Gallup polls, 97 percent of Americans answer "Yes." Supported by such findings, commentators on contemporary American life are unanimous in asserting that all but an insignificant fraction of Americans believe in God.

Another prevalent judgment about religious life in this country is that all Americans are coming to believe pretty much in the same things. The primary feature of American religion today seems to be no longer its diversity—based on the existence of several hundred Christian bodies—but its unity of outlook. Furthermore, the recent series of denominational mergers has fostered rising hopes for a general ecumenicalism.

Will Herberg in his now famous book, *Protestant-Catholic-Jew*, speaks of the "common religion" of America; the differences between Protestant denominations he considers to be organizational and ethnic rather than theological, and far outweighed by the consensus of beliefs. Robert Lee, in the *Social Sources of Church Unity*, suggests that a "common core Protestantism" exists because our urban, mobile, national society has broken down old parochial religious boundaries.

The major arguments have shifted away from whether this convergence in American religion has taken place, to the question of whether it is a blessing or a curse. Some churchmen contend that the homogenization of belief portends a loss of religious concern and authenticity; some social scientists condemn it as another symptom of the moral corrosion of mass society and the "O.K. world" of suburban complacency. On the other hand churchmen and social scientists hail the sloughing off of old divisions as symbolic of a new era of brotherhood, in which all can unite in a common quest to ennoble the human spirit.

We believe this debate is much too premature. We mean to raise a much more basic question: Have such changes really taken place? Is there really a "common core" belief in American Protestantism? Do the 97 percent of Americans who believe in God believe in the same God?

Our extensive survey shows that there are still a great many basic differences of belief among Protestant denominations in America.

The notion that American religion has undergone doctrinal agreement rests on two main premises:

□ That the old disputes (such as adult versus infant baptism) have lost their force and relevance; that nobody much believes in, or cares about, the idiosyncracies that once rent Christendom.

□ That the demise of these historic differences leaves Americans in general agreement, sharing in the essential core of Christian (and Judaic) teachings. That is, Americans now are in consensus on such bedrocks of faith as the existence of an all-powerful, personal God, the moral authority of the Ten Commandments and the New Testament promise of salvation.

But systematic evidence supporting these premises has been extremely scanty. Important and sweeping assertions about American religion need more careful examination, and firmer evidence. So we shall draw upon empirical data from our study of Christian church members to see to what extent American religion really is homogeneous.

As noted at the outset, American adults report a virtually unanimous belief in God. But what do they believe about God? And to what degree do they believe?

Table I demonstrates definitely that Americans are anything but unanimous in their beliefs about God; and that the distinctions are not only sharp between individuals, but between denominations as well.

Only 41 percent of the Congregationalists indicated unquestioning faith in a personal God. (Table 1.) This rises to 60 percent of the Methodists, 63 percent of the Episcopalians, about 75 percent among the center denominations, and is virtually unanimous among Southern Baptists and members of the fundamentalist sects. Overall, 71 percent of the Protestants endorsed the orthodox position, as compared with 81 percent of the Roman Catholics.

The second line shows that most of those who rejected unquestioning faith did not hold a different image of God, but were uncertain in their belief. They conceived of a personal divinity, but had doubts about his existence. Denominational differences here too are marked: 34 percent of the Congregationalists doubted; but only 1 percent of the Southern Baptists.

The fourth question is especially interesting, for it indicates a different conception of God, rather than mere doubt. Again, contrasts are striking: 16 percent of the Congregationalists, 11 percent of the Methodists, 12 percent of the Episcopalians—and none of the Southern Baptists—sub-

Table I: Interpretation of Scriptures (% agreeing)

Belief in God	Congregationalists	Methodists	Episcopalians	Disciples of Christ	Presbyterians	American Lutherans	American Baptists	Missouri Lutherans	Southern Baptists	Sects	Total Protestants	Catholics
"Which of the following statements comes closest to what you believe about God?"												
I know God really exists and I have no doubts about it.	41%	60%	63%	76%	75%	73%	78%	81%	99%	96%	71%	81%
"While I have doubts, I feel that I do believe in God."	34	22	19	20	16	19	18	17	1	2	17	13
"I find myself believing in God some of the time, but not at other times."	4	4	2	0	1	2	0	0	0	0	2	1
"I don't believe in a personal God, but I do believe in a higher power of some kind."	16	11	12	0	7	6	2	1	0	1	7	3
"I don't know whether there is a God and I don't believe there is any way to find out."	2	2	2	0	1	*	0	1	0	0	1	1
"I don't believe in God."	1	*	*	0	0	0	0	0	0	0	*	0
No answer	2	*	1	4	*	*	2	0	0	1	1	1
Number of respondents	(151)	(415)	(416)	(50)	(495)	(208)	(141)	(116)	(79)	(255)	(2326)	(545)

Note: Asterisk denotes less than half of 1 percent. Some columns fail to sum to 100% due to rounding error. The number of respondents shown for each denomination in this table is the same for all other tables. American Lutherans include the Lutheran Church in America and the American Lutheran Church. Sects include The Assemblies of God, The Church of God, The Church of Christ, The Church of the Nazarene, The Foursquare Gospel Church and one independent Tabernacle.

stituted some kind of "higher power" for a personal God.

Two percent of the Congregationalists, Episcopalians and Methodists were agnostics, and 1 percent of the Congregationalists said they did not believe in God at all.

If the first four lines are added, then 98 percent of both Protestants and Catholics may be said to believe to some extent in some kind of God. Superficially, this supports the Gallup figures. But the Gallup poll implication of uniformity and piety are entirely misleading.

Gallup studies also report that American Christians are virtually unanimous in believing Jesus Christ to be the Divine Son of God. But this faith too needs to be qualified.

Table 2 shows important contrasts in belief in the divinity of Jesus. Denominational differences are virtually identical to those in the belief in God. Only 40 percent of Congregationalist had no doubts that "Jesus is the Divine Son of God." This rose abruptly to 99 percent of Southern Baptists. The toal Protestant figure is 69 percent versus 86 percent for Catholics.

Examining some of the other orthodox beliefs about Christ (Table 3) brought differences into even sharper focus. Only 57 percent of all Protestants believed it "completely true" that "Jesus was born of a virgin," compared to 81 percent of Catholics. But the differences between the purportedly "common core Protestants" was much more startling: only 21 percent of Congregationalists believed it, rising to a peak of 99 percent of Southern Baptists.

The Southern Baptists remain rockbound in their faith in Jesus for all questions. Was it "completely true" that "Jesus walked on water"? Here the firm believers in this miracle fell to a small minority of the large liberal denominations, and counted only half of all Protestants. Even the Catholics fell to 71 percent. But the Southern Baptists held at 99 percent.

Like the existence of God, the Saviorhood of Christ

Table 2:
Belief in the Divinity of Jesus

"Which of the following statements comes closest to what you believe about Jesus?"

	Congregationalists	Methodists	Episcopalians	Disciples of Christ	Presbyterians	American Lutherans	American Baptists	Missouri Lutherans	Southern Baptists	Sects	Total Protestants	Catholic
"Jesus is the Divine Son of God and I have no doubts about it."	40%	54%	59%	74%	72%	74%	76%	93%	99%	97%	69%	86%
"While I have some doubts, I feel basically that Jesus is Divine."	28	22	25	14	19	18	16	5	0	2	17	8
"I feel that Jesus was a great man and very holy, but I don't feel him to be the Son of God any more than all of us are children of God."	19	14	8	6	5	5	4	0	0	*	7	3
"I think Jesus was only a man, although an extraordinary one."	9	6	5	2	2	3	2	1	1	*	4	1
"Frankly, I'm not entirely sure there was such a person as Jesus."	1	1	1	0	1	*	0	0	0	0	1	1
Other and no answer	3	3	2	4	1	0	2	1	0	1	2	2

Table 3:
Additional Beliefs About Jesus

	Congregationalists	Methodists	Episcopalians	Disciples of Christ	Presbyterians	American Lutherans	American Baptists	Missouri Lutherans	Southern Baptists	Sects	Total Protestants	Catholics
"Jesus was born of a virgin." Completely true	21%	34%	39%	62%	57%	66%	69%	92%	99%	96%	57%	81%
"Jesus walked on water." Completely true	19	26	30	62	51	58	62	83	99	94	50	71
"Do you believe Jesus will actually return to the earth some day?"												
Definitely	13	21	24	36	43	54	57	75	94	89	44	47
Probably	8	12	13	10	11	12	11	8	4	2	10	10
Possibly	28	25	29	26	23	18	17	6	0	1	20	16
Probably not	23	22	17	12	12	6	6	4	1	2	13	11
Definitely not	25	17	11	6	8	7	5	1	1	3	10	12
No answer	3	3	6	10	3	3	4	6	0	3	4	4

causes mixed reactions among American Christians. On the promise of the second coming of Christ ("Do you believe Jesus will actually return to the earth some day?") the differences between the Protestant denominations were far greater than that between Protestants as a whole and Catholics. A sizable majority of Congregationalists felt that Jesus would "definitely" or "probably" not return, compared to only 2 percent of Southern Baptists. Only 13 percent of Congregationalists and 21 percent of Methodists thought he would "definitely" return—compared to 75 percent of Missouri Synod Lutherans and 92 percent of the unshakeable Southern Baptists. Less than half of Protestants as a whole, as well as Catholics, thought the second coming "definite," and less than 60 percent thought it probable. Protestants can no longer sing, "Christ crucified, risen, coming again," with one voice, since less than half of total American Christendom really believes it true.

Table 4 deals with two basic religious beliefs about deity.

□ "There is a life beyond death." On this central tenet of Christianity only 36 percent of Congregationalists thought the statement "completely true," along with 49 percent of Methodists, and compared to 97 percent of Southern Baptists.

□ The controversial statement "The Devil actually exists" brought on a much wider spread of Protestant opinion. Only 6 percent of Congregationalists and 13 percent of Methodists consider Satan's existence certain, against 92 percent of Southern Baptists. Overall, 38 percent of Protestants and 66 percent of Roman Catholics were certain.

Unlike the supernatural, sin is related directly to the nature of man. Acceptance of man as sinful by nature increases in the usual pattern (Table 5), from the more liberal denominations on the left to the more conservative ones on the right; however, compared to differing beliefs

Table 4: Life Beyond Death and Belief in the Devil

	Congregationalists	Methodists	Episcopalians	Disciples of Christ	Presbyterians	American Lutherans	American Baptists	Missouri Lutherans	Southern Baptists	Sects	Total Protestants	Catholics
"There is a life beyond death."												
Completely true	36%	49%	53%	64%	69%	70%	72%	84%	97%	94%	65%	75%
Probably true	40	35	31	32	21	23	19	10	3	4	24	16
Probably not or definitely not true	21	13	13	0	7	5	7	4	0	2	9	5
"The Devil actually exists."												
Completely true	6	13	17	18	31	49	49	77	92	90	38	66
Probably true	13	15	16	34	17	20	17	9	5	5	15	14
Probably not or definitely not true	78	66	60	38	48	26	29	10	1	5	43	14

Table 5: Sin

	Congregationalists	Methodists	Episcopalians	Disciples of Christ	Presbyterians	American Lutherans	American Baptists	Missouri Lutherans	Southern Baptists	Sects	Total Protestants	Catholics
"Man can not help doing evil."												
Completely true	21%	22%	30%	24%	35%	52%	36%	63%	62%	37%	34%	22%
Probably true	36	36	34	36	35	30	28	20	14	15	31	29
Probably not or definitely not true	39	38	31	38	25	15	27	13	22	42	30	43
"A child is born into the world already guilty of sin."												
Completely true	2	7	18	6	21	49	23	86	43	47	26	68
Probably true	2	4	7	2	7	12	9	4	3	3	6	10
Probably not or definitely not true	94	87	71	90	68	37	65	9	55	46	65	19

in the supernatural, the spread is generally more even.

But on the acceptance of "original sin" ("A child is born into the world already guilty of sin"), there are some abrupt departures from the spectrum: those denominations with a liturgical or "high church" tradition are readily distinguishable by their willingness to accept this belief. Original sin cannot be absolved by personal efforts, but only through the church, especially those churches which emphasize ritual. Thus, the ritualistic Episcopalian church stands out sharply from the liberal group, and the American Lutherans from the other center groups. The strongly ritualistic Catholic church contrasts greatly with the Protestants in general, 68 percent to 26 percent.

It is clear that a general relationship exists between belief in original sin and theological conservatism, so that Lutherans are much more likely to hold this view than Episcopalians; yet the marks of the formal doctrine show up all across the table. Thus, on the left of the table the traces of old doctrinal differences on original sin may still be detected, while on the right these differences retain much of their old force.

What of the central concern and promise of all Christianity: salvation?

FAITH. Christians have long battled over the question of whether faith and works were necessary to be saved; but there has been no argument that faith at least was absolutely required. The central tenet of this required faith is belief in Jesus Christ as the divine son of God who died to redeem men from their sins. Some Christian traditions hold that more is necessary ("Faith without works is dead"); but all agree that there is no salvation outside of Christ.

However, we have seen that members of American denominations do not all believe Jesus divine. Therefore, it is not surprising to find them also disagreeing over whether belief in Christ is absolutely necessary for salvation.

In the liberal groups, only a minority consider faith in Christ "absolutely necessary." (Table 6) Among the conservative and fundamentalist groups, however, there is almost complete consensus about the necessity of faith in Christ for salvation. Overall, 65 percent of Protestants and 51 per cent of Roman Catholics gave this answer.

It seems likely that among all Protestant groups, persons who accept the promise of eternal salvation beyond the grave are also likely to feel that this eternal reward is contingent upon belief in Christ as savior.

All denominational groups are less likely to feel that one must hold "the Bible to be God's truth" in order to be saved. Overall, the pattern follows the now familiar increases from left to right, with one notable exception. The Southern Babtists had been most unanimous in their assertion of traditional Christian positions, yet they are not importantly different from the center on the importance of Bible literalism. This probably reflects the great emphasis they put on Christ as the primary source by which one attains grace.

WORKS. Having become accustomed to increases from left to right in proportions of those holding faith necessary for salvation, it comes as a surprise to see these trends reverse in Table 7.

Table 7 deals with the necessity of works. Those denominations weakest on the necessity of faith for salvation are the strongest on the necessity of "doing good for others." In fact, the proportions of people on the left who think doing good for others is required for salvation is higher than those of the same groups who think faith in Christ absolutely necessary. More people in the liberal churches believed in the absolute necessity of doing good than believed in life after death. On the other hand, the conservative groups do not give "good deeds" any special

Table 6: Requirements for Salvation: Faith

	Congregationalists	Methodists	Episcopalians	Disciples of Christ	Presbyterians	American Lutherans	American Baptists	Missouri Lutherans	Southern Baptists	Sects	Total Protestants	Catholics
"Belief in Jesus Christ as Savior." Absolutely necessary	38%	45%	47%	78	66%	77%	78%	97%	97%	96%	65%	51%
"Holding the Bible to be God's truth." Absolutely necessary	23	39	32	58	52	64	58	80	61	89	52	38

Table 7: Requirements for Salvation: Works

	Congregationalists	Methodists	Episcopalians	Disciples of Christ	Presbyterians	American Lutherans	American Baptists	Missouri Lutherans	Southern Baptists	Sects	Total Protestants	Catholics
"Doing good for others" Absolutely necessary	58%	57%	54%	64%	48%	47%	45%	38%	29%	61%	52%	57%
"Loving thy neighbor" Absolutely necessary	59	57	60	76	55	51	52	51	41	74	58	65
"Tithing" Absolutely necessary	6	7	9	12	10	13	16	7	18	48	14	10

Table 8: Barriers to Salvation: Improper Faith

	Congregationalists	Methodists	Episcopalians	Disciples of Christ	Presbyterians	American Lutherans	American Baptists	Missouri Lutherans	Southern Baptists	Sects	Total Protestants	Catholics
"Being completely ignorant of Jesus as might be the case for people living in other countries."												
Definitely prevent salvation	3%	7%	3%	8%	11%	15%	17%	36%	41%	32%	14%	4%
Possibly prevent salvation	13	23	16	38	24	29	31	28	39	46	25	24
"Being of the Jewish religion."												
Definitely prevent salvation	1	3	3	8	7	16	7	31	25	23	10	1
Possibly prevent salvation	6	9	10	18	12	16	25	23	28	33	15	11
"Being of the Hindu religion."												
Definitely prevent salvation	1	5	4	10	14	20	14	40	32	37	15	2
Possibly prevent salvation	12	11	12	28	15	22	25	16	27	31	17	13

Table 9: Barriers to Salvation: Improper Acts

	Congregationalists	Methodists	Episcopalians	Disciples of Christ	Presbyterians	American Lutherans	American Baptists	Missouri Lutherans	Southern Baptists	Sects	Total Protestants	Catholics
"Drinking liquor."												
Definitely prevent salvation	2%	4%	2%	0%	2%	2%	9%	1%	15%	35%	8%	2%
"Practicing artifical birth control."												
Definitely prevent salvation	0	0	2	2	1	3	1	2	5	4	2	23
"Discriminating against other races."												
Definitely prevent salvation	27	25	27	34	22	20	17	22	16	29	25	24
"Being anti-Semitic."												
Definitely prevent salvation	23	23	26	30	20	15	13	22	10	26	21	20

importance in the scheme for salvation.

We suggest that these responses on "doing good" by those who essentially reject the traditional notion of salvation represent their desire to ratify the ethical components of their religious outlook. Indeed, ethics are likely the central component of their religious beliefs.

Turning to the matter of tithing, it is clear that Christians in general are not inclined to connect this with salvation. Only 14 percent of the Protestants and 10 percent of the Roman Catholics thought tithing absolutely necessary.

To sum up: marked contrasts do exist among Christian denominations in their conceptions of what is required for salvation.

IMPROPER FAITH. If faith in Christ is essential for salvation, what acts and beliefs are an absolute barrier to it? Looking at the data in Table 8, those denominations strongest on requiring faith in Jesus for salvation are also strongest on rejecting salvation for non-Christians. However, in all denominations there were many who held faith in Christ to be absolutely necessary who were also unwilling to deny that persons outside the Christian faith could be saved. For example, only 14 percent of the Protestants and 4 percent of the Catholics said that "being completely ignorant of Jesus, as might be the case for people living in other countries," would definitely prevent salvation. Among Protestants, the proportion varied from a mere handful of Congregationalists, Methodists, Episcopalians and Disciples of Christ to 36 percent of the Missouri Lutherans, and 41 percent of the Southern Baptists. However, an additional and sizable group of Christians were somewhat inclined to accept this view. Twenty-five percent of the Protestants and 24 percent of the Roman Catholics thought ignorance in Jesus would "possibly prevent" salvation.

Jews, of course, are not "completely ignorant" of Jesus. Can they be saved? Relatively few thought it impossible for a Jew to be saved: only 10 percent of all Protestants and 1 percent of Catholics. Again, however, there were great contrasts among Protestant groups. One percent of the Congregationalists and 3 percent of the Methodists and Episcopalians took this position, while 31 percent of the Missouri Lutherans and 25 percent of the Southern Babtists saw no hope for Jews. A sizable group thought it "possible" that a Jew could not be saved, and taken together, more than half of the members of the more fundamentalist groups at least doubted the possibility of a Jew's salvation.

In summary, a substantial minority of American Christians consider persons in non-Christian religions as beyond the hope of salvation.

IMPROPER ACTS. American Christians no longer regard drinking as a certain road to damnation (Table 9). Only 8 percent of Protestants and 2 percent of Catholics thought it was. Only among the Baptists and the followers of fundamentalist sects did more than a handful attach temperance to their scheme of salvation.

Virtually no Protestants (only 2 percent) thought the practice of artificial birth control would prevent salvation, but perhaps even more interesting and surprising, less than a quarter of the Catholics held this view. Whether or not Catholics approve of birth control, more than three-quarters of them are unwilling to agree it carries the supreme penalty of damination.

The last two items in Table 9, dealing with racial discrimination, seem especially interesting, and repeat the pattern of evaluation of good works. On virtually all other "barriers to salvation," the conservative and fundamentalist bodies have been most likely to see them as absolutely necessary. However, on questions of racial discrimination and anti-Semitism, the Southern Baptists are the least likely of all religious groups to see them as relevant to salvation. Thus, while 17 percent of the Southern Baptists thought cursing would definitely prevent salvation, only 10 percent of them viewed anti-Semites as disqualified from entrance into God's Kingdom, and only 16 percent saw racial discrimination as a definite barrier. On the other hand, while only 13 percent of the Congregationalists thought that taking the name of the Lord in vain would definitely prevent salvation, 27 percent thought that racial discrimination and 23 percent that anti-Semitism would be barriers. Perhaps an even more suggestive contrast appears when we consider that about half of the members of all denominations thought it necessary to "love thy neighbor."

To sum up the findings on salvation: Christian denominations in America differ greatly in their beliefs about what a man must do to be saved. While most denominations give primary importance to faith, the liberal Protestant groups are inclined to favor good works. Protestants in a ritualistic tradition and Roman Catholics place greater emphasis on the sacraments and other ritual acts than do those from low-church traditions.

To return to the questions posed at the beginning of this article: Is religion in modern America accurately characterized as unified? Do such concepts as "common core Protestantism," and "common American religion" bear any important resemblance to reality?

We suggest that they do not. Differences in the religious outlooks of members of the various denominations are both vast and profound. On the basis of our data it seems obvious that American religion has indeed undergone extensive changes in recent decades, but it seems equally obvious that these changes have been greatly misperceived and misinterpreted.

Has American religion become increasingly secular? As noted, many commentators claim that the mystical and supernatural elements of traditional Christianity have been replaced by a demythologized (ethical rather than theological) religion.

In light of the data, important changes of this kind have indeed occurred to some American denominations. We have no comparable data on the past; but compelling historic grounds exist for assuming that the typical Episcopalian or Congregationalist in the mid-19th century firmly believed such tenets as the Virgin Birth and the Biblical miracles. If true, obviously secularization has indeed taken place in these religious bodies, for only a minority of them adhere to these beliefs today. On the other hand, among the Southern Baptists and the various sects, commitment to traditional Christian theology has been virtually impervious to change. The fact that these more evangelical and traditionalist denominations have been growing at a faster rate than the mainline denominations suggests that two simultaneous and divergent trends have been taking place:

□ Many people have been staying with or turning to "old-time" Christianity.

□ Others have been, to some extent, changing their theological outlook away from the supernatural and miraculous toward a more naturalistic view.

These trends seem to hold significant implications for the future.

Historically, the schemes in Christianity were largely marked by subtle doctrinal distinctions, and disagreements on proper ritual or organization. All observers generally agree that these issues have lost much of their relevance and divisive potential in contemporary America. Our data confirm these jugments.

But the data also suggest that new and generally

unnoticed splits have appeared in Christianity that may well hold greater potential for division than the old disputes.

Earlier disagreements were bitter; nevertheless they took place among men who usually shared belief in such basic components of Christian theology as the existence of a personal and sentient God, the Saviorhood of Christ, and the promise of life-everlasting.

But today, our data indicate, the fissures which map what might well be called the "New Denominationalism" fragment the very core of the Christian perspective. The new cleavages are not over such matters as how to properly worship God—but whether or not there is a God it makes any sense to worship; not whether the bread and wine of communion become the actual body and blood of Christ through trans-substantiation, but whether Jesus was divine at all, or merely a man. These disagreements, it must be emphasized, are not only between Christians and secular society, but exist within the formal boundaries of the Christian churches themselves.

How, therefore, can we account for all the hope and talk about general ecumenicalism? For those groups close together to begin with, such a possiblilty may well exist. At least there seem no overwhelming theological barriers to merger. But how are we to interpret exploratory talks between Roman Catholics and Episcopalians, or between Methodists and Baptists? Do the participants in the ecumenical dream simply misperceive one another's theological position, or do they consider such matters unimportant? Perhaps both of these factors are operating; but there are also signs that church leaders are becoming more aware of the doctrinal chasms that separate them.

Apparently most general ecumenical rhetoric comes from the most secularized mainline denominations. Probably the theological changes in these bodies have been accompanied by a lessening of concern for theology itself. Therefore, they may not view theological barriers as especially significant. But it is not true that the conservative groups are similarly unconcerned about doctrine. A good illustration comes from the relations between the National Council of Churches and fundamentalist bodies. Fundamentalists continually and bitterly denounce the National Council; yet it retains its composure and continues to encourage these hostile groups to become members.

Note that those bodies least amenable to the idea of ecumenicity are those which have the greatest consensus in religious belief. Among Southern Baptists and the various sects, for example, from 90 to 99 percent take similar positions on major articles of faith.

In bodies most concerned about ecumenicity, however, such as the Congregationalists and Episcopalians, members tend to be spread across a wide range of views on theology. Looking at these apparent conflicts on Doctrine, the question rises: How do the liberal bodies manage to remain united? Examination of the data suggests several reasons:
☐ Persons in the more liberal bodies place considerably less importance on religion and on their own church participation than do members of the more conservative bodies.
☐ Persons in the liberal bodies who do hold traditional beliefs have many friends in the congregation, while persons with more secularlized outlooks report that most of their friends are outsiders.
☐ The sermons preached in these denominations tend to be topical and ethical rather than doctrinal, while confessions and other rituals retain traditional form and content.

Thus it seems possible that the orthodox minority could remain unaware that the majority do not share their beliefs because the people they know in the congregation, their friends, do share these beliefs. Meanwhile, the majority, not being linked into the congregation by friendship bonds, may remain largely unaware of the fundamentalist segment of the congregation.

These factors may largely prevent potential conflicts from coming into the open. There are recent signs, however—such as the rise of theologically conservative lay groups within the more liberal denominations and the current growth of "tongues speaking" groups—that strains are developing even in these bodies because of theological differences.

One further fact ought to be mentioned. The liberal bodies that have most transformed their doctrines generate the least participation and concern among their members. By a strikingly wide margin, proportionately fewer attend worship services, join church organizations, pray privately, or believe in the importance of religion in their daily lives. Even within these more secularized denominations, those members who retain an orthodox theological outlook are consistently the more active in the life of the church. Probably, therefore, if a denomination is going to adopt new theological froms, it may have to find new organization and ritual forms as well, or run the risk of becoming less significant in the lives of men. Mission societies, the Ladies Aid, and other traditional church activities may be inappropriate and even distasteful to those who bring an ethical rather than a theological concern to the church, and who are perhaps more interested in social betterment than world-wide conversion. Such persons may also be more attracted to sermons raising moral questions about social problems than in messages of peace of mind in Christ. In any event, the churches are presently failing to obtain much participation from members with the most modernistic religious views.

At least four and probably five generic theological camps can be clearly identified among the American denominations. The first, the *Liberals*, comprises the Congregationalists, Methodists and Episcopalians, and is characterized by having a majority of members who reject firm belief in central tenets of Christian Orthodoxy. It is likely that the changes that have gone on in these bodies, since they are among the highest status and most visible Protestant groups, have largely produced the impressions that Protestantism in general has shifted toward a secular and modernized world-view.

The second group, the *Moderates*, is composed of the Disciples of Christ and the Presbyterians. This group is less secularized than the Liberals, but more so than the *Conservatives*, who are made up of the American Lutheran group and the American Babtists. The *Fundamentalists* include the Missouri Synod Lutherans, the Southern Baptists and the host of small sects.

Because of historic differences with Protestantism, the Roman Catholics are perhaps properly left to form a fifth distinct group by themselves. But on most theological issues, both those presented here and many more, the Roman Catholics consistently resemble the Conservatives. Only on special Protestant-Catholic issues such as Papal infallibility (accepted by 66 percent of the Roman Catholics and only 2 percent of the Protestants) were the Catholics and Conservatives in any extensive disagreement.

Merging the denominations to form these five major groups is the greatest degree of clustering that is statistically permissible. It seems very unlikely that ecumenical clustering could result in fewer.

Finally, the data seriously challenge the common practice of contrasting Protestants and Roman Catholics. Protestant-Catholic contrasts are often large enough to be notable (and often, too, remarkably small), but they seem inconsequential compared to differences found among the Protestant groups. The overall impression of American Protestantism produced when members of all denominations are treated as a single group (the "Total Protestant" column in the tables) at best bears resemblance to only a few actual Protestant denominations. Indeed, in some instances these "average Protestants" do not closely correspond to *any actual* denomination.

When we speak of "Protestants," therefore, we tend to spin statistical fiction. It seems unjustified to consider Protestantism as a unified religious point of view in the same sense as Roman Catholicism. Not that Roman Catholicism is monolithic either—clearly there are several theological strands interwoven in the Catholic church—but at least it constitutes an actual, organized body. Protestantism, on the other hand, includes many separate groups and the only possible grounds for treating them collectively would be if they shared a common religious vision. This is clearly not the case.

November/December 1965

A Protestant Paradox —
Divided They Merge

JEFFREY K. HADDEN

Discussion of mergers and increased cooperative efforts of the major Protestant denominations in recent years are without precedent. While the significance of these events has perhaps been overshadowed by the historic Vatican Ecumenical Council, the Protestant ecumenical dialogue is certainly a major contribution to what has the appearance of being the most significant development in Christendom since the Reformation. Analysis of ecumenicism in the United States have given a variety of interpretations to recent trends, but a predominant explanation is the assumption that differences among the various faiths are disappearing.

This assumption of emerging doctrinal unity has been challenged by Charles Y. Glock and Rodney Stark, sociologists from the Survey Research Center of the University of California, Berkeley. In their study "Is There an American Protestantism?" Glock and Stark conclude:

The new cleavages are not over such matters as how to properly worship God—but whether or not there is a God it makes any sense to worship; not whether the bread and wine of communion become the actual body and blood of Christ through transubstantiation, but whether Jesus was divine at all, or merely a man.

They found in matters as basic as belief in God more diversity among laymen of various Protestant denominations than between the "average" Protestant and the "average" Catholic. There was as much as a 70 percent difference between denominations in their belief in some doctrines. No single doctrine even approached unanimous acceptance.

But the Glock and Stark study covered only the laity. Some important questions remained concerning the beliefs of ministers and their influence in ecumenicism. For example, do the ministers also hold the broad expanse of beliefs found among the laymen, or do the clergy share a core of doctrine that makes the ecumenical movement possible? Also, are there other factors which may illuminate the increasing cooperation among denominations?

To obtain some answers, I recently surveyed ministers of six major Protestant denominations. Basically, I found the same wide diversity of creeds among them. But at the same time, the study indicates some other sources of religious unity deeper than doctrinal beliefs, which may have important implications for the current ecumenical movement.

The six denominations can be roughly classified in the same basic grouping established by Glock and Stark in their study of laymen:

LIBERAL: the Episcopal and Methodist churches
MODERATE: Presbyterian U.S.A.
CONSERVATIVE: American Baptist and American Lutheran
FUNDAMENTALIST: Missouri Synod Lutheran

Data for the study were gathered in early 1965 by a mail questionnaire. The 524 questions covered a wide range of subjects including doctrine and social issues. The questionnaire was sent to a probability sample of more than 10,000 parish and campus clergymen in the denominations. The over-all response rate was approximately 70 percent. The data in this article are based on the 7,441 returns from parish ministers.

These clergymen were asked to respond to belief statements; the six response categories were strongly agree, agree, probably agree, probably disagree, disagree and strongly disagree. The percents agreeing reported here combine the first two responses, strongly agree and agree.

This analysis begins with the minister's views of the role of the Bible in understanding the essence of Christian faith.

The response of clergy to four statements regarding the interpretation of the Bible dramatically illustrates that contemporary Protestant ministers substantially disagree in matters as basic as the use of the Bible. While Missouri Synod Lutherans are most obviously in radical disagreement, the distance between the others cannot be easily dismissed.

For example, immediately apparent is a wide range between the denominations in their interpretations of scripture. Only 11 percent of the Episcopal clergy said they believe in literal or nearly literal interpretation. Only one of five Methodist and Presbyterian ministers adhere to a literal interpretation. In contrast, the proportion believing in such an interpretation increases to 43 percent for American Baptists and American Lutherans. The Missouri Synod Lutherans are 67 percent points away from the Episcopalians, with almost four out of five stating that the Bible is to be interpreted literally.

The next statement in the table ("Adam and Eve were

Table 1: Interpretation of Scriptures (% agreeing)

"I believe in a literal or nearly literal interpretation of the Bible."

Methodist	18	American Baptist	43
Episcopalian	11	American Lutheran	43
Presbyterian	19	Missouri Synod Lutheran	78

"Adam and Eve were individual historic persons"

Methodist	18	American Baptist	45
Episcopalian	3	American Lutheran	49
Presbyterian	16	Missouri Synod Lutheran	90

"Scriptures are the inspired and inerrant Word of God not only in matters of faith but also in historical, geographical and other secular matters."

Methodist	13	American Baptist	33
Episcopalian	5	American Lutheran	23
Presbyterian	12	Missouri Synod Lutheran	34

"An understanding of the language of myth and symbol are as important for interpreting biblical literature as history and archaeology."

Methodist	77	American Baptist	62
Episcopalian	88	American Lutheran	62
Presbyterian	76	Missouri Synod Lutheran	34

individual historic persons") indicates that when the general issue of literal interpretation is put into a specific context, the interdenominational differences are even greater. Only 3 percent of the Episcopalians believe literally in the Genesis account of creation, compared with 90 percent of the Missouri Synod Lutherans. Episcopalians were separated from Methodists by only 7 percentage points on the first, general statement but by 15 percentage points on the second, specific statement.

The ministers also responded to six statements about these aspects of literalist doctrine: the physical resurrection of Christ, the virgin birth of Jesus, life after death, hell, the devil, and original sin. They are significantly split on all these points. The spread between Methodists and Missouri Synod Lutherans is no less than 42 percentage points on the virgin birth, and ranges as wide as 69 points on original sin. Furthermore, it becomes increasingly apparent here that denominations are split internally as well. Adherence to the doctrine of the virgin birth ranges from 40 percent among Methodists to 56 percent among Episcoplians and American Baptists. Acceptance of the literalist position approaches consensus only within the two Lutheran churches. Of the Missouri Synod Lutherans, 91 percent or more interpret all six statements literally, and at least 75 percent of the American Lutherans agree.

Note that the Methodists have replaced the Episcopalians as the most liberal denomination on these issues. Where the Episcopalians were the most liberal in rejecting literal interpretation of scripture, fewer Episcopalians than Methodists are willing to reject literalist doctrine. On four of the six statements, the Episcopal clergy are more conservative than the Presbyterian. Seventy percent of the Episcopalians accept the physical resurrection of Jesus, a greater proportion than Baptists. Thus, more Episcopalians are likely to reject the principle of literalism on selected issues, particularly the miraculous resurrection of Christ. But they are more inclined toward a literalist position than several other denominations.

On the earlier question of how the scriptures are to be interpreted, Baptists and American Lutherans were close together; on actual interpretation of doctrine, the American Lutherans stand nearer the fundamentalist Lutherans, and the Baptists nearer the moderate Presbyterians.

While Glock and Stark's laity study and my survey of ministers cover many of the same theological issues, the wording of the questions does not permit a direct

Table 2: Interpretation of Traditional Doctrine (% agreeing)

"I believe that the virgin birth of Jesus was a biological miracle."

Methodist	40	American Baptist	56
Episcopalian	56	American Lutheran	81
Presbyterian	51	Missouri Synod Lutheran	95

"I accept Jesus' physical resurrection as an objective historical fact in the same sense that Lincoln's physical death was a historical fact."

Methodist	49	American Baptist	67
Episcopalian	70	American Lutheran	87
Presbyterian	65	Missouri Synod Lutheran	93

"I believe in a divine judgment after death where some shall be rewarded and others punished."

Methodist	52	American Baptist	71
Episcopalian	55	American Lutheran	91
Presbyterian	57	Missouri Synod Lutheran	94

"Hell does not refer to a special location after death, but to the experience of self-estrangement, guilt, and meaninglessness in this life."

Methodist	58	American Baptist	35
Episcopalian	60	American Lutheran	22
Presbyterian	54	Missouri Synod Lutheran	6

"I believe in the demonic as a personal power in the world."

Methodist	38	American Baptist	67
Episcopalian	63	American Lutheran	86
Presbyterian	53	Missouri Synod Lutheran	91

"Man by himself is incapable of anything but sin."

Methodist	36	American Baptist	40
Episcopalian	45	American Lutheran	73
Presbyterian	47	Missouri Synod Lutheran	95

comparison of all responses. In addition, the survey of laymen used a four-point response scale, ranging from "completely true" to "definitely not true," and my study of clergymen used a differently worded six-point scale. Nevertheless, three statements are nearly parallel, permitting some comparison. These deal with the virgin birth, the devil, and the innately evil nature of man. (See Table 3.)

The results show a remarkable similarity on these items between laity and clergy within each denonimation. Although the figures seem to indicate that the clergy are more liberal than laity, I would hazard only cautious comparisons because of the dissimilarities between our studies and because of the small number of questions.

More important is the evidence that the liberal-to-fundamentalist order of denominations among ministers corresponds to that found among laymen by Glock and Stark. The Episcopal and Methodist clergymen, like laymen, are the most liberal. The Missouri Synod Lutheran clergy, like laymen, are the most fundamentalist. The few deviations that occur in the middle denominations involve only a few percentage points.

The data so far presented strongly support Glock and Stark's conclusion that new denominationalism does not have a common-core creed. Theological issues that divide laity also divide clergy, and with approximately the same magnitude. Thus, whatever the reasons for increasing interdenominational cooperation, ecumenicism does not appear to emerge from any growing doctrinal unity.

My figures, however, are for a single point in time, so there is no way of knowing how far apart the denominations under consideration were, say, 25 years ago. While never an adequate substitute for a study over time, an examination of different age groups may provide us with some clues as to possible changes in theological views. If there is any basis for the thesis of emerging doctrinal unity, we would expect to find younger ministers, irrespective of denomination, moving toward a consensus on doctrinal issues.

Table 4 presents the responses of clergymen by age

Table 3: Comparison of Belief Statements of Laity and Clergy

	Methodist	Episcopalian	Presbyterian	Am. Baptist	Am. Lutheran	Missouri Synod Lutheran
VIRGIN BIRTH						
Laity—"Jesus was born of a virgin." (% answering "completely true")	34	39	57	69	66	92
Ministers—"I believe that the virgin birth of Jesus was a biological miracle." (% answering "definitely agree")	28	40	36	58	68	90
DEVIL						
Laity—"The devil actually exists." (% answering "completely true")	13	17	31	49	48	77
Ministers—"I believe in the demonic as a personal power in the world." (% answering "definitely agree")	21	38	30	49	66	78
EVIL NATURE OF MAN						
Laity—"Man cannot help doing evil." (% answering "completely true")	22	30	35	36	52	63
Ministers—"Man by himself is incapable of anything but sin." (% answering "definitely agree")	19	25	25	22	53	72

Table 4: Age and Interpretation of Scriptures

	Age	Episcopalian	Methodist	Presbyterians	Am. Baptist	Am. Lutheran	Missouri Synod Lutheran
"I believe in a literal or nearly literal interpretation of the Bible." (% agreeing)	under 35	5	11	14	27	24	72
	35–44	11	16	16	41	43	73
	45–54	15	23	23	55	60	79
	over 55	14	23	31	47	74	84
"Adam and Eve were individual historic persons." (% agreeing)	under 35	0	9	11	20	28	85
	35–44	2	17	11	43	47	88
	45–54	6	24	22	59	72	92
	over 55	5	26	27	55	77	98
"Scriptures are the inspired and inerrant Word of God not only in matters of faith, but also in historic, geographic, and other secular matters." (% agreeing)	under 35	4	8	6	17	6	63
	35–44	2	12	9	30	26	74
	45–54	9	15	17	41	32	85
	over 55	8	17	21	42	50	90
"An understanding of the language of myth and symbol are as important for interpreting biblical literature as history and archeology." (% agreeing)	under 35	95	83	82	75	82	41
	35–44	89	78	83	64	55	35
	45–54	88	73	72	54	46	28
	over 55	81	68	58	57	46	28

groups to statements on interpretation of scripture. This table reveals an unambiguous movement by the younger ministers toward a nonliteral interpretation of the scriptures. In each denomination, younger ministers make more liberal interpretations of scripture. The only deviations in this pattern occur in the two groups over 45 years old, and these are minor. However, comparison of the absolute differences among Episcopalians, a liberal denomination, and among Missouri Synod Lutherans, a fundamentalist one, indicates that the theological position of the youngest and oldest within each are not far apart, the youngest ministers being somewhat more liberal than their elders in each denomination.

Examining the youngest and oldest clergymen across the six denominations on each statement disclose that the youngest are closer together than the oldest. On each of the four Bible interpretation statements, the percentages separating the youngest groups of ministers from each other are only about half those separating the oldest. For example, on literal interpretation (first statement), only 9 percentage points separate the youngest Episcopalian and Presbyterian ministers, while 17 separate the oldest. Moreover, the younger Baptist and American Lutheran ministers appear to be moving toward the liberal denominations at an even more rapid pace. For example, on the same issue, the under-35 group of American Lutheran ministers are only 19 percentage points from the corresponding Episcopal group while the over-55 American Lutherans are 60 points away from Episcopalians of the same age. The difference is even more dramatic on the third statement (the secular authority of scripture). Here the distance from the Episcopal position to the American Lutheran closes to 2 percentage points between the youngest ministers, while standing at 42 points between the oldest.

In sum, with the exception of the Missouri Synod Lutherans, younger clergymen are closer to agreement on the appropriate interpretation of scripture than older ministers. Furthermore, younger ministers tend to be closer to each other in biblical doctrine.

To interpret these findings as real change is, of course, somewhat tenuous: Ministers may become more orthodox as they grow older. Although possible, this does not seem probable. Older ministers who were educated in seminaries that were liberal 40 years ago are considerably more liberal than those who were educated in more literalist institutions. Thus, it would appear that this convergence does represent a genuine trend away from a literalist view of the Bible.

Turning to the question of liberalist doctrine, the hypothesis of emerging theological unity among the younger generation takes on a more complex motif in Table 5. While the youngest clergymen still tend to be more liberal than older ones, the former dramatic differences found between age-groups are no longer apparent. Only on the doctrine of the virgin birth (first statement) are the age groups widely divided. The difference is in the range of 15 to 20 percentage points for most denominations, with all younger ministers less likely to accept the doctrine. The only other statement where the young are clearly more liberal than the older ministers is the issue of judgment after death (third statement). But it is interesting here that those over 55 are slightly less likely to believe in divine judgment than those between 45 and 54. Furthermore, there is not much difference between the youngest and the oldest Episcopal and Missouri Synod Lutheran ministers. Note again that the Episcopalians and Methodists have switched positions as most liberal.

These figures introduce a perspective contrasting with

Table 5: Relationship of Age to Literalist Doctrine

Question	Methodist	Episcopalian	Presbyterian	Am. Baptist	Am. Lutheran	Missouri Synod Lutheran
"I believe that the virgin birth of Jesus was a biological miracle." (% agreeing)						
under 35	31	49	38	58	70	93
35-44	43	53	52	64	84	95
45-54	42	57	57	75	92	98
over 55	48	65	61	68	92	98
"I accept Jesus' physical resurrection as an objective historical fact in the same sense that Lincoln's physical death was a historical fact." (% agreeing)						
under 35	45	73	61	60	83	97
35-44	53	68	70	68	91	93
45-54	50	69	67	70	89	89
over 55	50	73	61	65	88	90
"I believe in a divine judgment after death where some shall be rewarded and others punished." (% agreeing)						
under 35	41	55	46	61	86	95
35-44	53	53	55	69	91	93
45-54	60	58	66	79	97	95
over 55	59	57	66	73	95	94
"Hell does not refer to a special location after death, but to the experience of self-estrangement, guilt, and meaninglessness in this life." (% agreeing)						
under 35	65	58	61	45	26	6
35-44	53	58	55	33	20	6
45-54	54	62	49	25	14	6
over 55	55	60	50	41	24	7
"I believe in the demonic as a personal power in the world." (% agreeing)						
under 35	34	67	49	57	80	91
35-44	38	65	50	64	88	93
45-54	41	63	59	77	91	89
over 55	40	58	57	70	91	90
"Man by himself is incapable of anything but sin." (% agreeing)						
under 35	39	47	49	37	71	85
35-44	34	45	47	33	69	85
45-54	35	44	46	45	78	86

the one on the interpretation of scripture. The younger ministers are more willing to reject a literal interpretation of the Bible and to introduce myth and symbol in understanding scripture, but they are not as willing to abandon specific doctrine. For example, the doctrine of the physical resurrection of Jesus (the second statement) remains almost as important to the youngest clergymen as to the oldest. Only 5 percentage points separate the youngest and oldest Methodist, Baptist, and American Lutheran ministers. The proportion of young and old believing in physical resurrection is the same among Presbyterians and Episcopalians, and even greater among the young Missouri Synod Lutherans.

The convergence of belief among younger ministers in interpreting scripture, then, largely disappears on specific doctrinal issues. In fact, among the liberal and moderate denominations the difference separating the younger ministers of each is greater on four of the six statements than it is for the oldest age groups. Younger ministers tend to be about as close or closer to older ministers of their own age in other denominations. Thus, denominationalism appears to be significant in determining what a minister actually believes about traditional theology.

While these results strongly suggest that denominationalism greatly influences a minister's theological outlook, the differences within denominations cannot be ignored. On almost every issue, the Methodists are about equally divided in acceptance or rejection of the traditional position. A third or more of the Presbyterians and Baptists each reject a strict literalism. Only in the two Lutheran denominations do ministers approach a consensus of creed. The sources of diversity within denominations need more careful analysis.

These findings have several implications for the current

ecumenical movement. Some observers have ascribed it to an emerging belief in a common core of American Protestantism. This assumption was previously challenged by Glock and Stark's study.

They argue that should ecumenicism be central to contemporary Protestantism, little concern for the old disputes like infant baptism and the virgin birth would be found; new awareness of Christian unity would appear instead. But no such unity was found. They suggested two possible interpretations of their findings, which, like mine, stand in sharp contradiction to the accelerated pace of ecumenical discussion and make difficult any explanation of its progress and prospects. Glock and Stark concluded:
□ The denominations simply may not realize the extent of their disagreement on basic doctrine. If so, negotiations aimed at unification may break down sooner or later.
□ Concern with theological issues as such may be lessening. Doctrinal barriers may not be seen as especially significant.

However, there remains the question of what other factors may illuminate the sources of ecumenicism. My findings so far point to three tentative observations:
□ First, the denominations are widely divided concerning doctrinal issues, in the pulpit as well as in the pew. Consequently, the ecumenical movement proceeds not from any doctrinal unity, but in spite of it. Protestants are divided; the age of their spiritual leaders makes little difference.
□ Second, all the denominations except the Lutherans have a substantial body of clergymen who reject dogmatic literalist theology. It seems appropriate to speculate that this more liberal group is leading efforts toward ecumenical cooperation. Having rejected a dogmatic literalist theology, these liberal ministers may stand ready to cooperate with others of different theological traditions

in pursuit of common goals.

□ Third, the essence of the ecumenical spirit may have little to do with doctrinal matters.

This study throws no light directly on ecumenical leadership, but it indicates that the theologically more liberal are more open to communication with traditions differing from their own. Table 6 shows the relationship between biblical literalism and three attitude statements dealing with doubt and unbelief. This index of biblical literalism was constructed from the six traditional doctrinal statements on page 65 dealing with the virgin birth and original sin. For each item, rejection of the literalist position was scored 0; uncertainty was given a value of 1; and acceptance of the literal interpretation of doctrine was scored 2. Thus, a score of 12 would represent the highest possible score on the index, and O would represent total rejection of the literalist position. In Table 6, literalism is classified as high, medium, or low.

The results are clear. Those who reject biblical literalism manifest considerable tolerance and understanding for those who live with doubts and uncertainty regarding their religious convictions. The unbeliever who is honestly seeking truth is admired more than those who are certain that they have completely grasped truth. The biblical literalist, on the other hand, is much more skeptical of the place of doubt in the Christian faith.

In sum, these results clearly indicate that tolerance of doubt and even unbelief is strongly related to rejecting literal interpretations of scripture. It would also seem probable that this same group would be more willing to tolerate interpretations of Christian doctrine different from their own. Although this study has no data on the clergy's involvement in ecumenical activities, the results suggest that such activity is highest among those who have strongly rejected biblical literalism.

Table 6: Literalism and Tolerance of Doubt and Ambiguity

Question	Biblical Literalism Index		
	Low	Medium	High
"Ambiguity and uncertainty as to what one is to believe and do are signs of faithlessness and indifference to God." (% agreeing)	6	12	25
"I would expect a thinking Christian to have doubts about the existence of God." (% agreeing)	71	56	38
"I have greater admiration for an honest agnostic seeking truth than a man who is certain that he has the complete truth." (% agreeing)	85	70	44

Table 7: Mission of the Church (% agreeing)

"The Christian church can only be its true self as it exists for humanity."

Methodist	75	American Baptist	75
Episcopalian	61	American Lutheran	74
Presbyterian	72	Missouri Synod Lutheran	71

"The primary task of the church is to live the Christian life among its own membership and activities rather than try and reform the world."

Methodist	6	American Baptist	8
Episcopalian	7	American Lutheran	10
Presbyterian	5	Missouri Synod Lutheran	12

"The church must speak to the great social issues of our day, or else its very existence is threatened."

Methodist	87	American Baptist	81
Episcopalian	80	American Lutheran	69
Presbyterian	84	Missouri Synod Lutheran	57

"The church should be taking a much more active role in the struggle for world peace."

Methodist	83	American Baptist	73
Episcopalian	76	American Lutheran	59
Presbyterian	77	Missouri Synod Lutheran	41

This leads to my third observation: The essence of the ecumenical spirit may have little to do with doctrinal matters. Unity may pivot on a common understanding of the church's place in contemporary society. Table 7 shows percentages of clergy agreeing with four statements regarding the mission of the church in the world. The first item states, "The Christian church can only be its true self as it exists for humanity." Admittedly, the statement is vaguely worded, and implementation may take a variety of forms, but denominational differences have virtually disappeared. With the exception of the Episcopalians, approximately three-quarters of the ministers respond affirmatively. The second statement (that the church ought to withdraw into itself rather than trying to reform the world) is strongly rejected by all denominations. Thus, there is virtual consensus that the church has a mission in this world.

The relationship of age to understanding the church mission (not presented here) indicates a somewhat greater commitment among the young ministers to church involvement. While differences do not disappear, young Lutherans—especially the American Lutherans—are more commited to an activist role for the church than are their elders.

These figures suggest that a major source of ecumenical unity stems from a consensus that the church has an activist responsibility in the world and that this mission may better be accomplished together rather than through the diversified energies of many groups. In other words, the sources of ecumenicism are social rather than doctrinal. Additional support for this thesis is seen in the data in Table 8.

The splits of new denominationalism run deep within and between churches on what the Christian position should be on many social issues. Disagreement ranges wide regarding church doctrine on urban problems and sexual relations. However, Protestant clergy agree that these are matters of concern for the church. This broadly based concern provides at least one major foundation for ecumenical discussion.

But beyond joint concern for current social issues, a heritage of Christian faith is also shared. Some men of the cloth may accept the supernatural interpretation of Christ's life and others reject it, but there is a common heritage professing the relevancy of Jesus for modern man. Regardless of how one views the sacred works of Christianity, all churchmen hold that the life and teachings of Christ fundamentally inform man in the appropriate relationships between God and man and among fellow men. This is not to say specific doctrine is irrevelant; the data presented here demonstrate the opposite. But apparently the roots of interdenominational cooperation go deeper than a common creed. The broad consensus is that God is both hidden and revealed in the life and the works of Christ. Since no one possesses the whole truth of Christian faith, tolerance of diversity becomes tenable. The earnest agnostic is more admired by our sample than the convinced dogmatist.

In a profound sense, the Christian religion is a faith professing a heritage which instructs men in the meaning of life rather than a dogmatic tradition proclaiming to possess ultimate reality. The sources of tolerance are many.

Christianity exists in an increasingly pluralistic world. Mass movements of people during the past 200 years have created mixed human communities. Television, magazines, and films have exposed the diversity of world views. Increasingly, Christianity exists in a world where it cannot impose its view on people aware of other persuasions. Freedom of religion increasingly means not only choice among a variety of faiths, but also freedom from religion.

The church has been forced to alter its doctrine to remain viable in a changing world. Ecumenicism, therefore, must certainly represent, on the one hand, the thrust of an institution for survival, and on the other, dramatic realization that doctrines that splintered the church are secondary to the common heritage—man's pursuit of the meaning of life, that which is beyond his empirical grasp.

Table 8: Social Sources of Ecumenicism (% agreeing)

"For the most part, the churches have been woefully inadequate in facing up to the civil rights issues."

Methodist	75	American Baptist	77
Episcopalian	70	American Lutheran	70
Presbyterian	76	Missouri Synod Lutheran	70

"Many whites pretend to be very Christian while in reality their attitudes demonstrate their lack of or misunderstanding of Christianity."

Methodist	79	American Baptist	84
Episcopalian	82	American Lutheran	80
Presbyterian	83	Missouri Synod Lutheran	78

"Christian education needs to bring laymen face to face with urban problems and propose solutions."

Methodist	74	American Baptist	67
Episcopalian	64	American Lutheran	68
Presbyterian	68	Missouri Synod Lutheran	64

"The churches should initiate inquiries into the implications of Christian convictions for the relations of the sexes, not assuming that there is any actual consensus in the churches on sexual morality."

Methodist	44	American Baptist	45
Episcopalian	44	American Lutheran	37
Presbyterian	51	Missouri Synod Lutheran	34

"The Christian is confined to no single method of gaining knowledge, but can make use of a plurality of methods relevant to the judgment to be made or the question under study."

Methodist	90	American Baptist	86
Episcopalian	94	American Lutheran	81
Presbyterian	90	Missouri Synod Lutheran	72

Will Ethics Be the Death of Christianity?

RODNEY STARK/CHARLES Y. GLOCK

Perhaps at no time since the conversion of Paul has the future of Christianity seemed so uncertain. Clearly, a profound revolution in religious thought is sweeping the churches. Where will it lead? Is this a moment of great promise, or of great peril, for the future of Christianity?

Some observers believe we have already entered a post-Christian era—that the current upheavals are the death throes of a doomed religion. Yet many theologians interpret these same signs as the promise of renewed religious vigor. They foresee the possibility of a reconstructed and unified church that will recapture its relevance to contemporary life. A great many others, both clerics and laymen, are simply mystified. In the face of rapid changes and conflicting claims for the future, they hardly know whether to reform the church, or to administer it last rites. Probably the majority of Christians think the whole matter has been greatly exaggerated—that the present excitement will pass and that the churches will continue pretty much as before.

Our own research, however, suggests that *the current religious revolution is being accompanied by a general decline in commitment to religion.*

The fact is that in the current debate about the future of Christianity there has been an almost total lack of evidence. The arguments have been based on speculation, hope and even temperament, but rarely on fact. Mainly this has been because so few hard facts about contemporary religion have been available. Our own findings do not entirely fill this vacuum. Still, what we have learned provides a number of clues about the trends in religious commitment, and permits a cautious assessment of the direction in which Christianity is headed. We have reached two main conclusions: that the religious beliefs that have been the bedrocks of Christian faith for nearly two millennia are on their way out; and that this *may* very well be the dawn of a post-Christian era.

While many Americans are still firmly committed to the traditional, supernatural conceptions of a personal God, a Divine Savior, and the promise of eternal life, the trend is away from these convictions. Although we must expect an extended period of doubt, the fact is that a demythologized modernism is overwhelming the traditional Christ-centered, mystical faith.

Of course, rejection of the supernatural tenets of Christianity is not a strictly modern phenomenon. Through the ages men have challenged these beliefs. But never before have they found much popular support. Until now, the vast majority of people have retained unshaken faith in the otherworldly premises of Christianity.

Today, skeptics are not going unnoticed, nor are their criticisms being rejected out of hand. For the modern skeptics are not the apostates, village atheists, or political revolutionaries of old. The leaders of today's challenge of traditional beliefs are principally theologians—

those in whose care the church entrusts its sacred teachings. It is not philosophers or scientists, but the greatest theologians of our time who are saying "God is dead," or that notions of a God "out there" are antiquated. And their views are becoming increasingly popular.

Although only a minority of church members so far reject or doubt the existence of some kind of personal God or the divinity of Jesus, a near majority reject such traditional articles of faith as Christ's miracles, life after death, the promise of the second coming and the virgin birth. An overwhelming majority reject the existence of the Devil. This overall picture, however, is subject to considerable variation among the denominations. Old-time Christianity remains predominant in some Protestant bodies, such as the Southern Baptists and the various small sects. But in most of the main-line Protestant denominations, and to a considerable extent among Roman Catholics, doubt and disbelief in historic Christian theology abound. In some denominations the doubters far outnumber the firm believers.

We are convinced that this widespread doubt of traditional Christian tenets is a recent development. What evidence there is supports this assumption. For if there has been an erosion of faith, we would expect many people to have shifted from denominations with unswerving commitment to that faith to denominations with more demythologized positions. Our data show that this is exactly what has happened. Because these denominational shifts indicate changes in religious outlook only indirectly, they do not *prove* our point. But they are very consistent with it.

More direct evidence of an erosion in orthodox belief is provided by contrasts in the percentages of orthodox believers in different age groups. Among people 50 years of age or older, we found that age made very little difference in the percentage subscribing to traditional beliefs. Similarly, among those under 50, orthodoxy differed little by age. But Christians over 50 are considerably *more* likely than younger people to hold orthodox views. The difference occurs in every denomination and is quite substantial.

These findings suggest that there has been an important generational break with traditional religion. The break consistently occurs between those who have reached maturity since the beginning of World War II—those who were 25 or less in 1940—and those who were raised in a pre-war America. In this as well as in many other ways, World War II seems to mark a watershed between the older America of small-town, rural, or stable urban-neighborhood living, and the contemporary America of highly mobile urban living.

Recent Gallup Poll findings indicate that the decline in American church attendance that began in the late 1950s is accelerating. This decline has been particularly sharp among young adults. The number who attend every week dropped 11 percent between 1958 and 1966. Futhermore, the Gallup interviewers found that Americans overwhelmingly believe that religion is losing its influence in contemporary life. In 1957 only 14 percent of the nation's Christians thought religion was losing its influence and 69 percent thought it was increasing; ten years later, 57 percent thought religion was losing ground and only 23 percent thought it was gaining. This would seem to mark an enormous loss of confidence in religion during the past decade.

Aside from this statistical evidence, there are numerous more obvious signs that a religious revolution is taking place. The radical changes in the Roman Catholic Church flowing from the reforms of Pope John XXIII and Vatican II are perhaps the most dramatic indications. Of equal significance is the ecumenical movement. Prevailing differences in doctrinal outlook still impede the unification of

Christian denominations. But though such differences seemed to preclude all prospects of unification several generations ago, today doctrinal barriers have broken down enough so that some mergers have already taken place, and clearly more are in the offing.

The mergers are taking place among denominations with the least residual commitment to traditional faith. More traditional denominations still resist the prospects of ecumenism. Thus it seems clear that a loss of concern for traditional doctrine is a precondition for ecumenism. And this in turn means that the success of ecumenism today represents a trend away from historic creeds.

These major signs of the depth and scope of religious change are accompanied by a spate of minor clues: the popularity of Anglican Bishop John A.T. Robinson's *Honest to God* and Harvey Cox's *The Secular City;* the widespread discussion of the "death of God" theology in the mass media; and the profound changes in the Westminster Confession recently adopted by the Presbyterian Church. All of these are compelling evidence of ferment. Nor is this exclusively a Protestant phenomenon. Almost daily the press reports nuns leaving their orders because they believe they can pursue their missions more effectively outside the church. Priests advocate "the pill." The number of Catholics taking up religious vocations has dropped sharply. Catholics ponder Teilhard de Chardin as seriously as Protestants reflect on Dietrich Bonhoeffer, the German theologian imprisoned and executed by the Nazis. A leading Jesuit theologian is quoted in *Newsweek* as admitting, "It is difficult to say in our age what the divinity of Christ can mean."

The seeds of this revolution were planted a long time ago. Since Kierkegaard, the "death of God" has been proclaimed—although subtly—by the theologians who have counted most. It is only because what they have been saying privately for a long time is now being popularized that the religious revolution seems such a recent phenomenon. For example, during the recent attempts to try him for heresy, Episcopalian Bishop James A. Pike defended himself by saying he had merely told the laity what the clergy had taken for granted for years. Moreover, the majority of Episcopalian church members hold theological views quite similar to Bishop Pike's. This presents an ironic picture of Sunday services in many churches. Both pastor and congregation reject or at least doubt the theological assumptions of the creeds they recite and the rituals in which they participate, but neither acknowledges this fact.

The heart of the religious revolution is the demise of what has been proclaimed as the core of Christian faith for nearly 2,000 years: a literal interpretation of the phrase "Christ crucified, risen, coming again." Now, in many theological circles both the fact of the current revolution and its demythologizing character are considered obvious. But what many consider obvious is, in this instance, terribly important—perhaps vastly more important than contemporary churchmen recognize.

In most of the commentary on the major transformations of our religious institutions, the key terms are change, renewal and improvement. Churchmen view the massive change in belief that is taking place not as a transition from belief to unbelief, but as a shift from one form of belief to another. The theologians who are leading this procession do *not* regard themselves as pallbearers at the funeral of God. It is *not* the end of the Christian era that they expect, but the dawn of a new and more profound period of Christianity.

The subtleties of what is being proposed in place of the old beliefs seem elusive, however. As sociologists, we find it difficult to imagine a Christian church without Jesus Christ as Divine Savior, without a personal God, without the promise of eternal life. The "new breed" of theologians, as we understand them, are telling us we are wrong—that we rigidly identify Christianity with an old-fashioned fundamentalism that modern Christianity has long since discarded. Still, we find it difficult to grasp the substance of their alternatives. Conceptions of God as utlimate concern, as love, as poetry, as the divine essence in all of us—the ground of our being—have powerful esthetic and rhetorical appeal. But how do they differ from humanism? And more important, how can such conceptions induce the kind of commitment necessary to keep the church, as an organization, alive?

For some contemporary churchmen, the new theology does mean the eventual abandonment of today's church and its replacement by a still vaguely defined spiritual community. But the vast majority of clerics expect no such thing. They expect the new theology to be effectively accommodated in the present church. They recognize that this accommodation will require some changes in the church's present organization and modes of operation, but they think that these changes *can* be made.

So far, the new theology has not altered the basic structure, form or functioning of the institutional church. The churches continue to predicate their structure and activities upon a conception of a judging, personal, active God, whether or not the theological views predominant among clergy and laity still conceive of God in these terms. Historically, the central concern of the churches has been the relationship between man and God. Part of their efforts have been directed to propitiating this active God, to teaching what must be done to escape his wrath and obtain his blessings. Such common religious terms and phrases as "praise," "worship," "seeking comfort and guidance," "bringing the unconverted to faith," and "seeking forgiveness for sins" all presuppose the existence of a conscious, judging God who intervenes in human affairs. An elaborate conception of God and his commandments is the raison d'être for church worship services, mission societies, adult Bible classes, baptism and communion.

Admittedly, there have been some superficial alterations. There have been various liturgical experiments. Sometimes the mass is recited in English rather than in Latin. Pastors have made some changes in the content of their sermons. But, by and large, the churches are still organized and conducted as they have been in the past. The traditional creeds are still recited—"I believe in God the Father almighty, maker of heaven and earth . . ."—and the old hymns regularly sung—"I Know that My Redeemer Liveth." There has been no substantial change in the sacraments. And, with some rare exceptions, there are no loud, or even soft, cries from the pulpit that Christ did not walk on water or that God does not see and hear all.

The general absence of institutional change does *not* mean that the clergy is more committed to traditional tenets than the laity. On the contrary, rejection of traditional Christian supernaturalism is perhaps even more widespread among the clergy than among the laity and follows essentially the same pattern of variation by denomination. Jeffrey K. Hadden's study comparing our findings on church members with national samples of clergy showed that laymen and clergymen in a given denomination are nearly identically distributed on questions of belief. For example, while 34 percent of Methodist laymen and 92 percent of Missouri Synod Lutheran laymen accept the virgin birth, 28 percent of Methodist clergy and 90 percent of Missouri Lutheran clergy accept this article of faith.

However, even if liberal ministers would like to alter the forms of the church on the basis of their new theology, they are not likely to find their congregations ready to permit it. This is because in all denominations supporters of the old theology still persist. What's more, they are likely to be their churches' most active laymen.

Thus the liberal pastor faces formidable restraints. His religious convictions might dispose him to reforms—to deleting, for example, references to traditional supernaturalism in the worship service, or to preaching the new theology from the pulpit and teaching it in Sunday school. But he is unlikely to have a congregation that would tolerate such changes. Even in congregations where orthodox members are in the minority such changes are unlikely. The minority will oppose them vigorously, while the plain fact is that the more liberal members are not likely to care much one way or the other.

This discrepancy between institutional inertia and theological revolution presents the churches with growing peril. Can the old institutional forms continue to draw commitment and support from people whose theological outlook is no longer represented in these forms—or at least maintain support until the theological revolution becomes so widespread that institutional changes are possible? More serious, can a Christianity without a divine Christ survive in *any* institutional form?

Our findings provide no final answer to these questions. They do, however, provide some important clues as to what will happen should future developments follow the present course. Evidently belief in traditional Christian doctrines, as they are now constituted, is vital to other kinds of religious commitment. While the churches continue to be organizsd on the basis of traditional orthodoxy, people who lack the beliefs that are needed to make such organization meaningful are falling away from the church. Today, the acceptance of a modernized, liberal theology is being accompained by a general corrosion of religious commitment.

Among both Protestants and Roman Catholics, orthodoxy is very strongly related to other aspects of religious commitment. (See Table I.) The highly orthodox are much more likely than the less orthodox to be ritually involved in the church, and they far surpass the less orthodox on devotionalism (private worship, such as prayer), religious experience, religious knowledge, and particularism (the belief that only Christians can be saved). Only on ethicalism among Protestants—the importance placed on "loving thy neighbor" and "doing good for others"—is the pattern reversed. By a slight margin, it is the least orthodox who are most likely to hold the ideals of Christian ethics.

Granted, it could be convincingly argued that devotionalism, religious experience, knowledge, particularism and perhaps even ritual involvement are not intrinsically necessary to the existence of Christian institutions. The fact that these forms of commitment decline as traditional belief declines could be interpreted as reflecting changes in modes of religious expression, rather than as an erosion of religious commitment. After all, the new theology implies not only a departure from old-time supernaturalism, but from religious practices that reflect supernaturalism. The clergy of the new reformation can hardly expect their adherents to break out "speaking in tongues."

But it is implausible to speak simply of change, rather than of decline, unless religious institutions retain a laity committed in *some* fashion. The churches cannot survive as formal organizations unless people participate in the life of the church and give it financial support. Without funds or members, the churches would be empty shells awaiting demolition.

This could just happen. (See Table II.) Among both Protestants and Catholics, church attendance is powerfully related to orthodoxy. Only 15 percent of those Protestants with fully modernized religious beliefs attend church every week, as opposed to 59 percent of those who have retained traditional views. Among Catholics, the contrast is 27 percent versus 82 percent. Similarly, the table shows that membership in one or more church organizations is strongly related to orthodoxy. Furthermore—and perhaps most important—financial support for the churches is mainly provided by those with orthodox views.

Table 1: Unorthodox Protestants Stress Ethics

As this table shows, both Protestants and Catholics who are highly orthodox are also the most likely to be ritually involved in the church, and to surpass the less orthodox in devotionalism (private worship, such as prayer); religious experiences (a mystical experience, or the like); religious knowledge; and particularism (the belief that only Christians can be saved). Among Protestants, however, the *least* orthodox are somewhat more likely to hold the ideals of Christian ethics.

| | Orthodoxy Index | | |
	Low	Medium	High
Percentage high on ritual involvement			
Protestants	19%	39%	71%
(Sample)	(595)	(729)	(705)
Catholics	19	36	55
(Sample)	(64)	(115)	(304)
Percentage high on devotionalism			
Protestants	20	49	79
Catholics	18	58	80
Percentage high on religious experience			
Protestants	25	57	86
Catholics	29	49	70
Percentage high on religious knowledge			
Protestants	15	19	46
Catholics	0	5	7
Percentage high on particularism			
Protestants	9	25	60
Catholics	15	28	40
Percentage high on ethicalism			
Protestants	47	46	42
Catholics	48	48	56

These findings show how the institutional church, predicated as it is on traditional theological concepts, loses its hold on its members as these concepts become outmoded. Consequently, if the erosion of traditional beliefs continues, as presumably it will, the church—as long as it remains locked in its present institutional forms—stands in ever-increasing danger of both moral and financial bankruptcy. The liberal denominations are particularly vulnerable because the demise of traditional theology and a concomit-

Table 2: The Orthodox Support the Church Most

It is the orthodox religionists, as this table shows, who attend church more, who belong to more than one church organization, and who contribute the most financially. This is why the fewer orthodox supporters the church has, the less its organizational support.

	Orthodoxy Index		
	Low	Medium	High
Percentage attending church every week			
Protestants	15%	31%	59%
Catholics	27	60	82
Percentage belonging to one or more church organizations			
Protestants	46	61	72
Catholics	14	24	46
Percentage contributing $7.50 or more per week to their church			
Protestants	17	23	44
Catholics	2	4	8
Percentage of Catholics who contribute $4 or more per week to their church	13	19	26

ant drop in other aspects of commitment is already widespread in these bodies.

In coming days, many conservative Christians will undoubtedly argue and work for an about-face. But it seems clear to us that a return to orthodoxy is no longer possible. The current reformation in religious thought is irrevocable, and we are no more likely to recover our innocence in these matters than we are to again believe that the world is flat.

Is there any way the impending triumph of liberal theology can be translated into the renewed church that liberal clergymen expect? Or must liberalism lead inevitably to the demise of organized faith? It is here the future is most murky. The alternatives to orthodoxy being advocated by the new theologians and their supporters are still rather formless. It is too soon to know just where they will lead. However, it seems clear that their central thrust is toward the ethical rather than the mystical.

This shift is more than a change in emphasis. The ethics of the new theologies differ sharply from the old. No longer are Christian ethics defined as matters of personal holiness or the rejection of private vices. They are directed toward social justice, toward the creation of a humane society. As theologian Langdon Gilkey put it recently, there has been a "shift in Christian ethical concern from personal holiness to love of neighbor as the central obligation. . . ." In the new ethical perspective, the individual is not neglected for the sake of the group, but the social situation in which people are embedded is seen as integral to the whole question of what is ethical. The long Christian quest to save the world through individual salvation has shifted to the quest to reform society.

Consequently, the new theology is manifested less in what one believes about God than in what one believes about goodness, justice and compassion. A depersonalized and perhaps intuitively understood God may be invoked by these theologies, but what seems to count most is not how one prepares for the next life—the reality of which the new theology seems to deny—but what one does to realize the kingdom of God on earth.

Among some modern Christians, ethicalism *may* provide a substitute for orthodoxy. Ethicalism is most prevalent in denominations where orthodoxy is least common. Furthermore, individual church members whose religious beliefs are the least orthodox score higher on ethicalism than the most orthodox.

But from an institutional point of view, is ethicalism a satisfactory substitute for orthodoxy? Can ethical concern generate and sustain the kinds of practical commitment—financial support and personal participation —that the churches need to survive?

If the churches continue their present policy of business as usual, the answer is probably No. The ethically oriented Christian seems to be deterred rather than challenged by what he finds in church. The more a man is committed to ethicalism, the less likely he is to contribute funds or participate in the life of the church. We suspect that, in the long run, he is also less likely to remain a member.

Tables III and IV show the joint effects of orthodoxy and ethicalism on financial contributions and church attendance. Table III shows that, among Protestants, the more a church member is committed to ethics, the less likely he is to contribute money to his church, regardless of his level of orthodoxy. The best contributors are those of unwavering orthodoxy, who reject the religious importance of loving their neighbors or doing good for others. A simliar relationship exists among Roman Catholics. Regardless of orthodoxy, the higher his score on the ethicalism index, the less likely a parishioner is to give money to the church. Member commitment to Christian ethics seems to cost the churches money.

Table IV shows the joint impact of ethicalism and orthodoxy on church attendance. Here again, among Protestants, it is clear that the higher their ethicalism, the less likely they are to attend church regularly. The best attenders are the highly orthodox who reject ethical tenets. Among Roman Catholics, it is unclear from these data whether or not ethicalism has any effect at all upon church attendance.

These findings were rechecked within liberal, moderate, and conservative Protestant groups, and within specific denominations as well. Invariably, a concern with ethics turned out to be incompatible with church attendance and contributions. Furthermore, these same relationships held true for participation in church organizations and activities.

Table 3: Who Contributes the Most Money?

Among both Protestants and Catholics the more a church member is committed to ethicalism—placing importance on "loving thy neighbor" and "doing good for others"—the less likely he is to give money to his church. The best contributors are those with unwavering orthodoxy and the least commitment to ethicalism.

	Ethicalism Index		
	High	Medium	Low
Protestants—Orthodoxy Index	Percentage who contribute $7.50 or more per week to their church		
High	38%	43%	58%
(Sample)	(304)	(240)	(111)
Medium	18	25	43
	(333)	(321)	(44)
	18	20	12
	(241)	(251)	(34)
Catholics—Orthdoxy Index	Percentage who contribute $4 or more per week to their church		
High	27	45	*
	(150)	(122)	(4)
Medium	16	18	*
	(48)	(56)	(4)
Low	7	21	*
	(30)	(28)	(1)

* Too few cases for a stable percentage.

Today's churches are failing to engage the ethical impulses of their members. Regardless of whether they retain orthodox religious views, to the extent that people have accepted Christian ethics, they seem inclined to treat the church as irrelevant. Obviously, this bodes ill for the future of the churches. It means that the churches have to find a substitute for orthodoxy that will still guarantee their organizational survival. And while *some* form of ethicalism might work as a theological substitute for orthodoxy, clearly the existing efforts along this line have not succeeded.

Table 4: Who Attends Church the Most?

Among Protestants, the higher the ethicalism, the lower the church attendance. The best attenders are the highly orthodox who do not stress Christian ideals. The data for Catholics are unclear.

	Percentage who attend church every week Ethicalism Index		
	High	Medium	Low
Protestants—Orthodoxy Index			
High	55%	58%	67%
(Sample)	(328)	(247)	(113)
Medium	29	31	52
	(347)	(331)	(44)
Low	19	22	10
	(255)	(165)	(39)
Catholics—Orthodoxy Index			
High	82	82	*
	(161)	(124)	(4)
Medium	65	60	*
	(51)	(57)	(4)
Low	30	27	*
	(30)	(30)	(2)

* Too few cases for a stable percentage.

Sooner or later the churches will have to face these facts. This will require a forthright admission that orthodoxy is dead. Furthermore, it will also require—and here's the real hurdle—a clear alternative. It will require a new theology, ethically-based or otherwise, and radical changes in forms of worship, programs and organization to make them consistent with and relevant to this new theology.

But even successfully fulfilling these tasks will not ensure the survival of the church. Indeed, the immediate effect will almost certainly be to alienate those members committed to old-time orthodoxy and thus to sharply reduce the base of support on which the churches presently depend. The gamble is that these people can be replaced by renewing the commitment of those members whose interest in the church is presently waning, and by winning new adherents among those who do not now belong to any church.

Clearly, among the conservative churches such a radical change of posture is not likely. The impact of modernized theology on these bodies has so far been indirect, in the loss of members who switch to more liberal denominations. To the extent that these losses remain endurable, the conservative clergy and laymen can continue to ignore the current crisis.

If institutional reforms are to come, the liberal churches must lead the way. Our findings suggest that not only are the liberal churches in the best position to make such changes, but that their existence may very well depend on their doing so.

At present, the liberal bodies are functioning as way stations for those who are moving away from orthodoxy, but who are still unwilling to move entirely outside the church. These new members may prove to be only a passing phenomenon, however, unless the liberal churches can find a way to *keep* them. And the churches' current organizing practices are clearly unequal to this task. For it is the liberal churches that are currently in the poorest organizational health.

Most liberal Christians are dormant Christians. They have adopted the theology of the new reformation, but at the same time they have stopped attending church, stopped participating in church activities, stopped contributing funds, and stopped praying. They are uninformed about religion. And only a minority feel that their religion provides them with answers to the meaning and purpose of life, while the overwhelming majority of conservatives feel theirs *does* supply such answers. The liberal congregations resemble theater audiences. Their members are mainly strangers to one another, while conservative congregations are close-knit groups, united by widespread bonds of personal friendship.

In the light of these facts, the liberal churches do not seem organizationally sound in comparison with the conservative ones.

Although all these signs point to the need for a radical break with traditional forms in the liberal churches, it seems quite unlikely that this will happen any time soon. For one thing, there is no sign that the leaders of these bodies recognize the situation that confronts them. Here and there one hears a voice raised within the clergy, but such spokesmen are a minority with little power to lead. What's more, leadership is not the only thing lacking. There is no clearly formulated blueprint for renovating the churches. The critical attack on orthodoxy seems a success, but now what? The new theologians have developed no consensus as to what they want people to believe, or as to what kind of a new church they want to build.

What we expect is that all of the Christian churches will continue a policy of drift, with a rhetoric of hope and a reality of business as usual. There will be more mergers and more efforts to modernize classical interpretations of the faith, but these will go forward as compromises rather than as breaks with the past. Perhaps, when the trends we see have caused greater havoc, radical change will follow. Institutions, like people, have a strong will to survive. But institutions do die, and often efforts to save them come too late.

Only history will reveal the eventual fate of Christianity. As matters now stand, there seems to be little long-term

Table 5: Liberal Churches May Be in Trouble

Compared with the conservative Protestant denominations, the liberal churches are in poor organizational health. Liberal religionists, as the table shows, attend church less, contribute less money, and have a generally weaker religious commitment. Still the liberals know more about religion than Catholics, and contribute more money to their church than Catholics.

	Members of liberal Protestant churches	Members of moderate Protestant churches	Members of conservative Protestant churches	Members of Roman Catholic parishes
Percentage high on orthodoxy	11	33	81	61
Percentage high on ritual involvement	30	45	75	46
Percentage high on devotionalism	42	51	78	65
Percentage high on religious experience	43	57	89	58
Percentage high on religious knowledge	17	25	55	
Percentage who feel their religious perspective provides them with the answers to the meaning and purpose of life	43	57	84	68
Percentage who attend church weekly	25	32	68	70
Percentage who have 3 or more of their 5 best friends in their congregation	22	26	54	36
Percentage who contribute $7.50 or more per week to their church	18	30	50	6

a Congregationalists, Methodists, Episcopalians.
b Disciples of Christ, Presbyterians, American Lutherans, American Baptists.
c Missouri Synod Lutherans, Southern Baptists, Sects.

future for the church as we know it. A remnant church can be expected to last for a time, if only to provide the psychic comforts that are currently dispensed by orthodoxy. But eventually sutstitutes for even this function are likely to emerge, leaving churches of the present form with no effective rationale for continuing to exist.

This is not to suggest that religion itself will die. As long as questions of ultimate meaning persist, and as long as the human spirit strives to transcend itself, the religious quest will continue. But whether the religion of the future will be in any sense Christian remains to be seen. Clearly it will not be, if one means by "Christian" the orthodoxy of the past and the institutional structures built upon that orthodoxy. But if one can conceive of Christianity as a continuity in a search for ethics, and a retention of certain traditions of language and ritual, then perhaps Christianity will survive.

The institutional shape of religion in the future is as difficult to predict as its theological content. Conceivably it may take on a public character, as suggested recently by sociologist Robert Bellah, or the invisible form anticipated by another sociologist, Thomas Luckmann. Or it may live on, in a form similar to the religions of Asia, in a public witness conducted by priests without parishes. Quite possibly, religion in the future will be very different from anything we can now expect.

The portents of what is to come could easily seem trivial today. William Butler Yeats, in a poem celebrating the slow death of ancient paganism and the coming birth of a still unformed Christianity, asked a question that we may well ask of our own religious future:

And what rough beast, its hour come round at last, Slouches towards Bethlehem to be born?

June 1968

FURTHER READING:

Religion in Secular Society by Bryan Wilson (London: C. A. Watts & Co.,1966). An analysis of secularization in Great Britain providing parallels with the American situation.

The Invisible Religion by Thomas Luckmann (New York City: Macmillan, 1967).

When Ministers Meet

C. DALE JOHNSON

Should I join the local ministers' association? Well, they're a good bunch of fellows and very fine Christian gentlemen, I'm sure. But I don't see what good it's going to do. Here you've got that Pentecostalist fellow, and then the Congregationalist, and the Methodist. And so they get together and what good can come out of it? Why they're miles apart; they can't even pray together decently. You get a watered-down kind of Christianity out of it, the lowest common denominator.

(A Missouri Synod Lutheran pastor)

Nearly all American clergymen subscribe to the values of brotherhood, cooperation, and tolerance—at least as abstract ideals—but this might be hard to discover from their attitude and behavior toward each other. Although Sunday sermons to their congregations may be full of the rhetoric of harmony, relations between clergymen generally tend to be diffident, occasionally even hostile. At

89

best, their contacts are infrequent—unless they belong to the same denomination.

There are three basic reasons why American clergymen fail to establish and maintain effective interdenominational contacts and cooperation:

□ Regardless of frequent and sometimes vehement assertions to the contrary, the clergy in any given community are usually in competition with each other for members. The high rate of residential mobility in contemporary society, together with the ease with which church membership can be acquired, changed, or dropped, tends to make a minister anxious about his prospects for retaining present members and attracting new ones.

□ The clergy represent different and often conflicting religious ideologies, traditions, and practices. It is not easy for a clergyman to accept as a peer another man of God who is "unqualified" or "in error" concerning vital matters, especially if the bishop or other ecclesiastical superior disapproves of such associations.

□ Many ministers and priests seem to have little enough time for even their most essential parish and denominational duties, and thus could not justify additional time for joint activities with other clergy. (Frequently this is at least in part a rationalization for failure to meet some of their felt obligations to the ideals of tolerance and cooperation.)

These observations are based on interviews with 147 ministers and priests in nine Midwestern cities and indicate that there are strong "occupational" inhibitions to establishing either friendships or colleague relationships across denominational lines. In fact, clergymen in the survey can be divided into three categories, according to the way they carry out their interdenominational relations: *professional* types, *priestly* types, and *prophetic* types.

The professional-type clergyman sees his colleague relationships in strongly interdenominational terms. He is tolerant of diversity, favorable toward interdenominational organizations, and supports establishment of a code of professional ethics. In these respects he is similar to professionals in other fields such as law or medicine, who have feelings of respect for the training and practice of a peer and a desire to further the profession—in spite of individual differences of opinion. Thus, he regards as colleagues any clergymen who are properly trained, technically competent in their work, and ethically responsible, and he is willing to discuss problems with other clergy, regardless of their denominations. Professionalism also characteristically involves some self-regulation by the professionals in such matters as recruitment and training of personnel, relationships among members, and relationships between members and the public at large. So the professional-type clergyman is an active participant in local and state ministerial associations. He promotes the ecumenical movement and sees most religious bodies, like his own, as sincere though imperfect expressions of the Christian faith. In theology, he often adheres to a liberal or neo-orthodox approach.

The priestly-type clergyman can regard as his proper colleagues only those who share his religious doctrines and beliefs and his ritualistic qualifications (ordination)—in other words, only clergy of his own denomination. He may manage friendly relations with others, but he cannot accept them as occupational peers because they are fundamentally "in error" and in other ways "unqualified." Thus he is unlikely to be deeply involved, if at all, in any interdenominational association of ministers or council of churches. Nor is he likely to favor regulation of his work by means of a code of ethics. His conduct already is adequately prescribed by the doctrine and legal rules of his church. Doctrinal orthodoxy, submission to higher ecclesiastic authority, and strongly sacramental ideology are the denominational characteristics of the priestly type.

The prophetic-type clergyman feels directly called by God to the work of the ministry. He determines his relationships with other clergy on the basis of their personal character and charismatic qualifications. Like the professional-type he tends to disregard denominational boundaries. But unlike him, the prophetic-type will also disregard training or technical competence. He will look for colleagues who, like himself, are divinely called and inspired, who are comitted to the "separate life" and to literal acceptance of the Word of God as revealed in the Bible. His relationships with professional or priestly clergymen will be unimportant to him. He will not be interested in interdenominational ministerial associations that include "modernists," "unbelievers," and those who regard the ministry as a "profession" rather than a "calling." Any professional code of ethics that deters him from trying to "save" members of other churches (the professional-type clergyman would call it proselytizing) would be clearly unacceptable. When faced with serious problems in his work, he will go to his charismatically endowed colleagues, not for consultation, but for help through collective prayer and meditation.

By no means did all ministers and priests in the survey fit neatly into one or another of the three types. With some ministers, incompatible elements of two or all of the types were clearly at war. The characteristics of the priestly type, for example, were almost never explicitly stated, but instead had to be partially inferred. For example, a Roman Catholic priest expressed his feeling about the local ministerial association this way:

No, I don't belong to the ministerial association. They asked me when I first came, but I said no. It's not that we're forbidden to belong or anything. There was a priest once who did belong to a group like this, and everybody

A TYPOLOGY OF MINISTERS

	PROFESSIONAL	PRIESTLY	PROPHETIC
AUTHORITY	Authority based on technical competence in the tasks of the ministry	Legal, traditional authority, charisma of office	Personal charismatic authority based on divine "call"
TRAINING	Critical, scholarly emphasis	Indoctrination and discipline	Training useless without the "call," superfluous with it
PREACHING	Topical preaching	Interpretive preaching on Biblical topics	Inspiration and archaic biblical literalism
SACRAMENTS	Symbols with possible pragmatic value	A means to grace	Only symbols
LITURGY	Flexible, pragmatic, possibly experimental approach to liturgical matters	Set liturgy in worship service; may overshadow or eliminate sermon	No set order of worship.
PASTORAL WORK	Emphasizes counseling	Emphasizes supervision and discipline with respect to ritual duties of parishioners	Emphasized conversion of the unsaved and supervision of members with respect to maintenance of taboos
INSTRUCTION	Instructs potential members in a few basic principles; no requirement of assent to creeds or doctrines	Requires long period of instruction in creeds and doctrines, as well as assent to them for confirmation	Instruction based on Bible; new members admitted on evidence of conversion
HIERACHY	Free professional, contractual relationship between self and clients (congregation)	Official in ecclesiastical bureaucracy	Member of a "fellowship"; not part of an organized hierarchy
THEOLOGY	Neo-orthodox or liberal	Orthodox	Fundamentalist

said, "Oh my, isn't that fine." What did he prove? I don't think he proved anything, and I like to believe that I'm not proving anything by staying away. We have our differences and pretending that we don't isn't going to change a thing.

This sort of attitude was frequently accompanied by refusal to participate in interdenominational worship services or public ceremonies where clergymen from other denominations were going to take part; refusal to allow any outside group, whether of a religious character or not, to use the church edifice; and refusal to cooperate in various attempts to improve the moral tone of the community (for example, campaigns to make the community "dry").

Frequently professionally oriented clergymen assessed the difficulties of establishing effective and harmonious colleague relationships in somewhat the same way as the Lutheran minister quoted above. They tended to remain optimistic, however, hoping to make the existing ministerial association stronger and to expand its functions.

In discussing their colleague relationships, some ministers used the term "fellowship," a standard cliché in contemporary Protestantism. The word was used more frequently by prophetically oriented ministers than the others. The following statement by the pastor of a small sectarian congregation is illustrative:

When I was out in the Bay area, I was a neighbor to Dr. B., an outstanding Presbyterian pastor. He, together with several other men, a Baptist, a Presbyterian, a Lutheran, a Mission Covenant, and myself and a couple of other Free Church pastors, began kind of a pastors' prayer fellowship. It was a rich experience. It did something to my ministry. . . . That fellow (Dr. B.) breathed the power of God. . . . One morning the Presbyterian came to prayer meeting all broken up. He said, "Men, I want you to pray for me. . . . I don't have a single layman in my church that I can call on for public prayer. Not one." He was really broken up about it. And we prayed that day for him and for his church. And a couple of months later he came all enthused. He said, "You know, God has answered our prayers, not with laymen but with young people." A complete spiritual awakening had taken place in his youth group.

Disregard of denominational lines and imputation of charismatic qualities are noteworthy in this account. Such statements were not uncommon responses from clergy of sectarian groups. Of course, priestly and professional-type clergymen participate in prayer fellowships too, but not as frequently as the prophetic types.

Because of their deliberate reliance on charismatic qualities, prophetic-type ministers usually did not approve of a code of ethics. However, the notion that a code of professional ethics for the clergy might be valuable had occurred to very few ministers before they were interviewed. Many summarily rejected the idea, apparently because this would negate the supra-mundane character of their calling. A typical negative response was:

> If all the pastors would just behave according to the spirit of Christian love, there would be no need for a code of ethics. Of course, if they don't have the spirit of Christian love, the code of ethics wouldn't help anyway.

Other clergy, believing that there are many concrete instances where it is unclear just what the spirit of Christian love specifically requires, said they would support an attempt to establish a code of ethics. They emphasized the need for a prohibition against proselytizing. It was obvious that some self-righteous ministers thought that other clergymen needed the guidance of a code. Though most ministers explicitly disapproved of the practice of luring members away from other congregations, many were not sure of the proper course of action in borderline cases.

For example, what should a minister do when members of another local congregation seek membership in his church? Many felt that such persons should be admitted on the same basis as anyone else. Others thought it necessary to inform the other minister and encourage the prospective members to return to their own church, or at least talk the matter over with their own minister. One pastor explained:

For one thing, handling it this way encourages trust and friendship in the relations among the ministers in the community. On the other hand, you have to consider the spiritual welfare of the people involved. Some people are chronically dissatisfied with their church membership no matter where they belong, and making it easy for them to change church membership rather than face up to their own spiritual problems does them a disservice.

This viewpoint is, of course, most likely to come from a professionally oriented clergyman who does not feel that he or his denomination has any monopoly on religious truth and value. Also this clergyman probably has no worries over declining membership. Some ministers who were quite disapproving of proselytizing nevertheless admitted to doing it. One said resignedly, "Let's face it; we're all sheep-stealers."

Conceivably, a code of professional ethics could be sponsored by a ministerial association. However, these associations rarely function on a high professional level. The members seem to have a hard time agreeing on anything except opposition to sin, and the more obvious kinds of sin at that.

The character of interdenominational organizations varied with each community. The larger the community, the more likely it was to have several somewhat specialized ministerial associations or their equivalents. For example, in one large metropolitan community, there were: a large ministerial association organized by the local council of churches; a "pastors' action group," which took fairly sophisticated action on such matters as the operation of a local correctional institution, liquor sale regulations, and segregation in housing; a local chapter of the National Association of Evangelicals providing "fellowship" for sectarian fundamentalists and pietistically oriented Lutherans and Presbyterians; and an all-Negro ministerial alliance.

In smaller communities, the ministerial association membership generally included most of the Protestant clergy, with the frequent exception of highly orthodox Lutherans. The ministerial association in a small community fulfills some of the functions performed by a council of churches in a larger community. It provides religious services at homes for the aged, correctional institutions, and mental hospitals; it supports community charities and arranges joint worship services on special occasions. More often than not, its secular action consists of attempts to eliminate, through pressure and publicity, such evils as automobile sales on Sunday, liquor, gambling, indecent movies, and obscene literature. Despite a tendency to concentrate on such matters, ministers' groups have also turned their attention in recent years toward major social problems and public policy.

When asked to explain the purposes of ministers' organizations, many clergymen replied, "Oh, it's purely social." Generally, priestly and prophetic types approved of this superficiality of the ministerial associations. In contrast, the professional-type ministers wished to see the organizations speak out on community affairs and enforce professional ethics.

In general, the prospects for development of strong interdenominational, professional-type colleague relationships in the near future are not favorable. This appears to be true despite the fact that common work problems and other common experiences have tended toward creation of an occupational subculture which crosses denominational boundaries. So far, however, the divisive forces have balanced the unifying ones and have effectively thwarted the vigorous efforts of those few clergymen working toward professional organization on an occupation-wide basis.

May/June 1966

The Marching Ministers

JEFFREY K. HADDEN/RAYMOND C. RYMPH

One afternoon in Chicago last June, a young white Episcopalian minister sat down in the middle of a busy intersection. Sitting with him and blocking traffic were 251 fellow civil rights demonstrators, Negro and white, protesting de facto segregation in Chicago's schools. As the police arrived and began making arrests, an officer approached the minister. "We don't want to arrest you," he said. "Get up and you can go." "No," said the minister, and sat firm. He was arrested.

White ministers so openly committed to the civil rights movement that they are willing to go to jail have received prominence in recent years. Some, like the Rev. James Reeb who was killed in Selma, Alabama, in 1965, have even died for their commitment. But the ministers who go to Selma or Jackson, or who participate in civil rights demonstrations in their own towns, add up to only a comparative handful. The vast majority of ministers, who may support the civil rights movement from their pulpits, repeatedly balk at active involvement. Why?

Do these men say one thing and believe another? Or is it, perhaps, a matter of not being "free" to act on their convictions? Perhaps the dictates of conscience yield to other voices. Are there influences from the governing board of a denomination and the attitudes of a congregation that control a minister's actions?

The young Episcopalian minister who was arrested for sitting down in the street had come to Chicago with 47 fellow clergymen to participate in an intensive study program at the Urban Training Center for Christian Missions. They were from 17 states and represented seven denominations —the Protestant Episcopal church, the United Church of Christ, the American Baptist church, the Moravian church, and three separate branches of the Lutheran church. The ecumenical program conducted by the Urban Training Center (UTC) was designed to equip these men to work in highly urban areas by informing them about, and involving them in, the political, social, and spiritual problems of the metropolis. They had come to learn firsthand about the kinds of problems represented by the street demonstrations over Chicago school segregation. The UTC staff unambiguously approved of their taking part in the demonstrations although it was stressed that the choice was an individual one. This situation provided an excellent opportunity for us to learn about the pressures and conflicts in their decisions to take part or not.

On Wednesday, June 9, the day before the first march, the UTC trainees were given a detailed briefing about the Chicago school situation. Their Thursday classes were suspended so they could participate in the protest. Most (40 out of 48) took part in the first march. By the end of three days, however, after several hundred arrests had occurred, the picture of civil rights involvement among the UTC ministers had altered sharply. Only half (25 out of 48) had become so deeply involved as to be arrested. The others gradually dropped out of the protest as the conflict between marchers and police became increasingly intense.

Demonstrations began on June 10, following a circuit court injunction prohibiting civil rights groups from carrying out a two-day school boycott to protest the rehiring of School Superintendent Benjamin Willis by the Board of Education. On that day, an estimated 400 persons marched from Soldier Field down the middle of Outer Drive to City Hall, where they staged a sit-in on LaSalle Street. There were no arrests.

The failure of the police to intervene in this obstruction of traffic was sharply and publicly criticized by Chicago's Mayor Daley. The following day, Friday, June 11, marchers again assembled at Soldier Field to march on City Hall. They complied with police requests to march in two lanes only. However, at an intersection in Grant Park, police surrounded the marchers and demanded that they walk in a single lane. This was contrary to the marchers' understanding of the ground rules for the march. In protest many of them sat down, and 252 were arrested. On Saturday, the marchers were stopped at State and Madison in the Loop, where 192 sat down and were arrested.

As already mentioned, 40 of the 48 UTC trainees marched on Thursday. On Friday, the number declined to 35. When the first arrest occurred on Friday, the ministers were given an extra opportunity by the police to get up and thus avoid arrest. Eleven of the marching trainees either did not sit down or got up when the police asked them to. The remaining 24 trainees sat down, refused to budge, and were arrested.

On Saturday, only 20 UTC trainees marched. (Five who had been arrested on Friday elected to remain in jail.) Eleven were arrested on Saturday, including one who had dropped out of the march when threatened with arrest on the previous day. The other ten were repeaters.

Thus 25 UTC trainees were arrested and 23 were not arrested. Who were the ministers willing to carry their commitment to the point of arrest? Why did others who professed essentially the same liberal beliefs balk at appearing in the public demonstrations, or drop out of the marches to avoid arrest?

Some of those not arrested were, no doubt, simply opposed to tactics of civil disobedience. Though sympathetic with Negro goals, they rejected law-breaking as a suitable means of achieving these goals. Ministers are traditionally committed to upholding the law, and, for some, this commitment might well have outweighed the commitment to civil rights. But intensive interviews indicated that this was, at best, a secondary reason why many of the UTC trainees refused to become involved to the extent of being jailed. We had to look elsewhere to explain their behavior.

Did the ministers' denominations have anything to do with the extent of their participation in the racial protests? We found that it definitely did. Of the five denominations with more than a single representative at UTC, two of them, the Episcopal church and the United Church of Christ, had repeatedly taken strong stands on civil rights. The other three denominations, all Lutheran, had taken stands considerably more modest in scope and less vigorous in actual implementation. This simple dichotomy between strong and moderate denominational commitment to civil rights were directly related to the involvement pattern of the minister-trainees.

Of the seven Episcopalians, only one was not arrested, and he was physically unable to march. Four of the six members of the United Church of Christ were arrested, and a fifth was away in Detroit speaking on the civil rights issue. The Lutheran denominations, on the other hand, had considerably smaller proportions arrested. Even with

the three Lutheran groups combined, only 14 out of 33—
that is, 42 percent—were arrested, in contrast to 75 percent
of the ministers from the more liberal denominations.

An even more important determinant, we found, was
the specific congregation's attitude on the civil rights
question. The UTC trainees tended to act in a way which
they perceived would be acceptable to their parishioners
at home.

That such considerations can mold a minister's behavior
was clearly and dramatically illustrated earlier in the
Little Rock school crisis of 1957. Of 29 Little Rock clergymen interviewed at that time by Ernest Q. Campbell and
Thomas F. Pettigrew *(Christians in Racial Crisis, 1959)*,
only five said they believed in racial segregation. Moreover,
by 1957 all of the major Protestant denominations had
adopted declarations commending the 1954 Supreme Court
decision on desegregation. Yet in spite of their personal
beliefs and the official backing of their denominations, the
white clergy of Little Rock by-and-large refused to take an
active stand in favor of civil rights during their city's racial
crisis. Why? There can be no doubt that they were restrained by the perceived opposition of their all-white,
segregationist congregations.

There are a number of ways in which a minister's congregation can bring strong pressures to bear on his conduct. The Little Rock minister who took a liberal stand on
desegregation stood to lose church members, financial support for his church, and possibly even his position. This
situation still prevails in many parts of the South, and the
minister in those areas who takes an aggressive stand on
Negro rights may well place his life's work, if not his life
itself, in jeopardy.

What about the Northern clergy, then? The past few
summers have witnessed repeated invasions of the South by
Northern ministers. (This has indeed been the only way

for the Protestant denominations to take an active role in the Southern civil rights conflict, since Southern ministers could not participate, for the reasons just outlined, without severely endangering the institutional strength of their churches there.) Are Northern ministers free from this sort of restraint? Unfortunately, no. The North has its own technique for creating de facto segregation in schools, jobs, and housing, as has been dramatically underlined by the recent racial explosions in cities such as Los Angeles, New York, Chicago, and Rochester.

Resistance by the congregation to ministerial involvement in the civil rights movement is, then, by no means limited to the South. Wherever a minister is directly responsible to an all-white congregation, there is the real possibility that he will be shackled by their direct or subtle opposition.

Probably few Northern congregations would have expressed strong opposition to their ministers milling in the crowd of 100,000 persons who descended on the nation's capitol in the summer of 1963, since this would constitute relatively low involvement in an event which was receiving wide popular support, including the encouragement of the President. But many of these same congregations would respond quite negatively to their pastor traveling a thousand miles to get arrested in a civil rights demonstration in Mississippi. This behavior might be criticized as prying into other people's business, committing an act of civil disobedience, associating with persons of dubious character, and neglecting the responsibilities of his parish.

For these reasons, clergymen in non-parish positions and those whose parishes are integrated should be freer to join in the struggle than those who are responsible to, and perhaps restrained by, all-white congregations. The pattern of participation by the UTC trainees in Chicago during the summer of 1965 solidly bears this out.

There were only four ministers from integrated metro-politan parishes among the UTC trainees, but all four were arrested. These four represented three different de-nominations, suggesting that their involvement was inde-pendent of denominational affiliation. Seven of the nine ministers in non-parish positions (or 78 percent) were arrested. These men were responsible only to denomina-tional officials or boards; it appears that the absence of a responsibility to a specific parish membership freed them to act according to their personal convictions. As for the two non-parish ministers who were not arrested, one came from the most conservative denomination represented at the training center, and the other was not in the city dur-ing the marches.

In significant contrast, nine of the ten ministers with white suburban parishes did *not* get arrested in the demon-strations; and the one who did expressed some ambivalence toward remaining in his current position. Four of these suburban ministers did not even march in the demonstra-tions. This almost universal pattern of noninvolvement is strongly reminiscent of the behavior in Little Rock.

Seven ministers (32 percent) of non integrated inner-city churches were arrested, thus occupying an intermediate position between ministers of inner-city integrated and sub-urban churches. We asked all 19 of these ministers how they felt the "influentials" of their congregations would re-act to the possibility of church integration. Of the 12 who were not arrested, two said that the influentials would be openly opposed to integration; five reported that the influ-entials would verbally go along with integration but would probably be pretty uncomfortable if Negroes actually came into the church; and three reported that the influentials would probably go along with "token integration" but re-sist a serious attempt to develop a truly integrated congre-gration. Of the seven who were arrested, only one felt that the influentials in his congregation were opposed to church integration. Three others were serving congregations with token integration. Thus these ministers also acted in accord with what they preceived to be their congregations' views on integration.

An intriguing question was raised by the fact that all six of the ministers from nonmetropolitan communities were arrested. Why? A plausible explanation may be derived from the unusual situation of small-town ministers receiving urban training at the request of their denominations. It may have been indicated to these men that they would soon be transferred to a metropolitan area. For that reason, they may not have concerned themselves too much about the attitudes of their small-town congregations.

A second possible explanation is the demographic structure of the nonmetropolitan areas. Except for the South, these areas have few, if any, Negroes. The problem of civil rights remains remote. Therefore, the minister's participation in a civil rights demonstration would be little more than an intellectual extension of a noninvolved "tolerance" for civil rights.

A third possible explanation for the nonmetropolitan minister's behavior is that, with few or no Negroes in the community, a civil rights sermon would probably draw little criticism from the congregation. This would lead the minister to conclude, perhaps erroneously, that the congregation supported his position.

But, independent of their personal convictions, why did the small-town ministers act unanimously and without hesitation? Did they not have some concern for their careers? It is possible that their career aspirations lay someplace other than the suburban church, a suggestion supported by a recent study of seminary students that indicated only 33 percent aspired to a parish situation. If these small-town ministers aspired to metropolitan or nonparish careers, then, far from being a detriment to their careers, the arrest might be worn as a badge of courage.

The age of the nonmetropolitan ministers offers still another possible explanation for their behavior. The average age of the nonmetropolitan ministers was 30.2 years compared with 38.0 for the total group, a difference of 7.8 years. Popular psychology and history have long linked youth to radical behavior. Thus, their active civil rights involvement may reflect the independence of youth, and a more critical attitude toward the existing social structure— qualities that have nothing to do with parish location. These men served nonmetropolitan parishes because such parishes were not the prize positions, and prize positions do not normally accrue to youth.

Another aspect of ministerial involvement is the question of participation inside or outside one's own community. When a minister participates in a civil rights demonstration in his own community, there is always the possibility that the power structure of the community may bring pressure upon his laity to initiate reprisals. This is less likely when the minister is participating in another community. Furthermore, it is easier for his congregation to view his behavior in a favorable light when he is not protesting against their own prejudices or the injustices of their own community.

Indeed, the local parish ministry of Chicago did not appear to be widely represented in the 1965 summer marches. Local ministers who marched tended to be one of three types: Negro ministers of Negro churches, white ministers of Negro churches, and nonparish ministers associated with seminaries and denominational offices. This impression of the Chicago situation is consistent with observations of civil rights activity in other areas. For example, in Little Rock during the 1957 desegregation crisis, Negro children were escorted through the hostile crowds to Central High School by seven clergymen. Five of these ministers were from out of town. This pattern appears to be fairly typical.

The UTC trainees in Chicago were, however, all from out of town. In that sense at least, all of them were free to participate in the demonstrations without immediate fear of reprisals from the laity. Still, many did not commit themselves to the point of arrest. And since the group was about evenly divided between those who chose arrest and those who did not, it is reasonable to assume that, with pressures operating in both directions, many of the trainees had a hard time making the decision about whether and to what degree to become involved. Most likely they discussed this decision with their fellow ministers—probably with their training center roommates (who had been assigned alphabetically, without regard for denomination), since they had not had time to become well acquainted with the others.

Our observations strongly suggest that the trainees were indeed influenced by their roommates' decisions. Of the 50 (including seminary students who had roommates), 32 acted just as their roommates did with respect to being arrested, and only 18 deviated from their roommates' behavior. Having a roommate who chose arrest probably made it easier for those in doubt to fully commit themselves.

The picture of the contemporary white Protestant minister which emerges from our observations of the UTC group in Chicago is of a man who cannot isolate himself or his decisions from the social context in which he moves. Contrary to the traditional image of the inner-directed minister with an ear only for the voice of conscience, the minister vis-a-vis the civil rights movement is a man who does—and must—listen to the voices of his denominational superiors, his congregation, and his fellow clergymen. He does not and cannot act solely on the basis of convictions.

In the case of the UTC trainees, the ministers who were

younger, who served integrated parishes or had nonparish positions, who belonged to denominations that had taken a strong stand on civil rights, and whose fellow ministers (specifically roommates) supported an active commitment to the Negro cause were *freer* to choose arrest than those who had the opposite characteristics. The others, regardless of private feelings, had more circumscribed choices.

Thus the decision of a Northern minister to go to Mississippi or of a Southern minister to speak up against discrimination in his own town—or, in reverse, that of a local clergyman in Little Rock or Chicago to ignore the abuses carried on in his own community—is a complex one in which personal belief plays only a part. For some, the road to active involvement in the civil rights struggle is barricaded by denominational or congregational resistance. For others, it is a road whose hazards are diminished by the comfort and support they receive from their churches, their parishioners, and their fellow clergymen along the way.

September/October 1966

III: INTERNATIONAL
PERSPECTIVES ON CONFLICT

Religion Is Irrelevant in Sweden

RICHARD F. TOMASSON

In 1544, the Swedish riksdag declared the Evangelical-Lutheran religion to be the official religion of the state. At the same time, it warned that anyone who opposed the state church would be "banished and regarded as a heretic and heathen." Yet today Sweden is a land tolerant in sexual matters and an advanced welfare state—as secular as any Western industrial country.

On an average Sunday, church attendance in Sweden is only 4 or 5 percent of the population. The number of clergymen is no more than it was two centuries ago, when the population was less than a quarter of what it is now. Compared with the United States, where church news and services are regularly carried by newspapers, radio, and television, religion is a scarce commodity in the Swedish mass media.

Still, there is little hostility among the Swedish people toward religion or toward the clergy. The school system is the only one in Western Europe which has established a universal policy of *objective* teaching of religion at all levels. About 90 percent of the Swedes continue to be baptized, confirmed, married, and buried by the church. And the majority claim they would join the church if it were disestablished—which is likely to happen in the 1970s. Thus, there is neither widespread participation in nor hostility toward the church. The prevailing attitude in Sweden is indifference.

Why is traditional religion so irrelevant throughout most of Swedish society, while in other Western countries —even in much of nearby Norway—it continues to command substantial support from the people? Before trying to answer this interesting question, let us first get a clearer picture of religion in modern Sweden—by examining what the Swedes feel and think about religion, and how religion influences them.

All Swedes—except for some 33,000 Catholics, 15,000 Jews, and a small number who have resigned from the church—are formal members of the Church of Sweden. This is more than 98 percent of the population. About 5 percent of the population also belongs to various "free churches"—Protestant sects emphasizing salvation, strict morality, and freedom of religion.

Attendance at Sunday mass in the state church has declined from 17 percent of the population in 1900 to 3.3 percent in 1962. Those who belong to the free churches are more likely to attend Sunday services and therefore they bring the overall attendance figure to 4 or 5 percent. Finland and Denmark have equally low patterns of Sunday church attendance. Attendance is probably lower in these three Scandinavian societies than in any other Western country. For Great Britain, average Sunday attendance is around 15 percent; for the United States, attendance is around 43 percent.

Sweden has 13 dioceses, and there is marked variation

among them in attendance at Church of Sweden services on Sunday. The urban diocese of Stockholm has the lowest attendance—1.1 percent. The diocese of Lulea—the most northern, rural, and most unevenly developed area in Sweden—has the highest: 6.3 percent, which is over twice the average attendance throughout Sweden(3.1 percent). Other surveys have indicated substantially higher percentages for church attendance but they have included ceremonies such as baptisms, weddings, and burials, the great majority of which are conducted under church auspices. Of course, church attendance is also considerably higher at Christmas and Easter. As might be expected, attendance is greater among the more traditional segments of the population: rural people, women, and the old, than among urban people, men, and the young.

The relationship between a Swede's social class and his church attendance is noteworthy. Table 1 shows the percentage of Swedes by class who attended religious services at least twice the month before the survey—a measure of the religiously committed. It is clear that the middle class participates more in organized religion than the working class and the upper class. Moreover, there are marked differences by class in participation in the Church of Sweden and in the free churches. The working class is the *least* likely to participate in the Church of Sweden. The upper class is the *least* likely to participate in the free churches.

Despite these low attendance records, the majority of Swedes say they believe in God—if not an orthodox Christian God, at least a deity who "oversees the world." In 1956, a study found that 52 percent of Swedish men 18 to 55, and 72 percent of Swedish women 18 to 55, believed in such a God. (See Table 2.) In the United States, by contrast, over 95 percent of the people say they believe in God. When these Swedes were asked whether they be-

Table 1: The Middle-Class Attends Church Most

Active participants in the Church of Sweden and the free churches, by social class (1955-56)

Attended church at least twice in previous month	Church of Sweden	Free Church	Total
Social group 1 (professionals, executives, university graduates)	10%	2%	12%
Social group 2 (white-collar workers small-business men, etc.)	10	8	18
Social group 3 (workers)	6	7	13
Number: 2579			

lieved in a "God who intervenes in my own life," the percentage answering Yes declined to 37 for men and 57 for women. Asked whether they thought that "believers will go to heaven," the percentages dropped to 22 for men and 36 for women. Asked "Do you try to be a real Christian?" only 26 percent of the men and 36 percent of the women answered Yes.

Table 2: The Majority of Swedes Say They Believe in God

Religious beliefs of Swedish men and women, 18-55 (1956)

Percentage who	Men	Women
"believe in a God who oversees the world"	52%	72%
"believe in a God who intervenes in my own life"	37	57
"believe that believers will go to heaven"	22	35
"try to be a real Christian"	26	36
Number: 1000 men 1000 women		

In Sweden, the word Christian tends to mean a person who is of the community of believers, not someone who behaves in a morally approved way, as it often does in the Anglo-American societies. Herbert Tingsten, a leading editor and political scientist, once said the great majority of Swedish Christians are Christians in name only, and went on:

"They say they believe in God, yet do not accept the doctrines that distinguish Christianity. They want to keep education in Christianity [in the schools] yet do not go to Church. Baptism, confirmation, marriage and burial—these are the contacts these people have, not with religion (for there is no reason to have such contact!), but only with the Church. The holy sacraments provide a setting for festive occasions. A necessity for this state of affairs is that they do not listen, do not understand, or at least do not pay any attention to what is said. They inquire as little into the meaning of these things as they ponder electricity on a journey by tram. This we all know, and this we all say—but the convention is so well established that it is considered a trifle unbecoming to say so publicly."

An individual's answer to the question whether he tries to be a real Christian or not is probably a good clue to how much he subscribes to orthodox Christian beliefs. Among Swedes, there is a remarkable variation by age in answers to this question. (See Table 3.) Some 35 percent of Swedes, age 12 to 15, say Yes. Then among Swedes 18 to 25, there is a decline to a low point of 18 percent saying Yes. (For men between these ages, the figure is only 15 percent.) The percentage increases consistently with age—70 percent of Swedes 56 and over answer Yes.

These figures, even in the absence of data for other societies, certainly indicate a low acceptance of orthodox Christian belief among the Swedes. While there is evidence that religious beliefs increase with age, in Sweden the

Table 3: The Generation Gap in Trying to Be a Real Christian

Answers to "Do you try to be a real Christian" by age, entire population (1955-56)

	Yes	Uncertain Don't know	No	Number
12-15	35%	41%	24%	289
16-17	20	36	44	91
18-25	18	20	62	320
26-35	24	27	49	366
36-45	31	27	42	375
46-55	38	24	38	356
56-	70	19	11	641

variation between the young and old is so great that another explanation is needed—namely, that in recent decades there has been a marked decline in religious belief. It is unlikely that when the 18-25 cohort reaches 56 and over, 70 percent of *them* will say they try to be real Christians. A study of the attitudes of over 2,000 Swedish youth 12-24 done in 1968 reveals that almost half unequivocally deny the existence of a deity. Results to the question "Do you believe there is a God?" were as follows:

22 percent Yes, absolutely; 31 percent Maybe, uncertain; 46 percent, there is not. In Stockholm 63 percent deny the existence of a God.

A sizable minority of Swedes continue to believe in a life after death, although substantially fewer than in most Western societies. In a 1960 poll, 40 percent of a national sample answered Yes to such a question. This percentage can be compared with those of seven other Western countries in which sample polls were taken at about the same time. The percentages believing in a life after death, in rank order were:

74 percent United States, 71 percent Norway, 68 per-

cent Canada, 63 percent Netherlands, 56 percent Great Britain, 55 percent Switzerland, 40 percent Sweden and, 38 percent West Germany. A Swedish report of this international study pointed out that in no other country were there so many uncertain answers as in Sweden: 37 percent gave Don't Know answers, and only 23 percent actually disclaimed belief in a life after death.

In 1964, a cross-section of Swedes 16 and over were asked how often they "pray to God." The results: 13 percent "daily," 13 percent "quite often," 27 percent "more rarely," 46 percent "never." By contrast, only 8 percent of a 1953 American sample claimed that they never prayed.

An important observation about religious belief in Sweden is the absence of much opinion that sees religion as the sole basis of morality. The same people who were asked about praying chose these alternatives about the relation between religion and morality:

☐ 16 percent "There is no other basis for morality than religion."

☐ 27 percent "For me personally religion is the only basis for morality, but I still believe that men can find another basis for moral behavior."

☐ 41 percent "Morality does not need to be based on religion."

☐ 16 percent "Do not agree with any of the above statements."

In the United States, on the other hand, religion is conventionally viewed not only as the basis of morality, but as the basis of the "American way of life" and of democracy. Similarly in England—more comparable with Sweden in having an established church—morality and democracy are conventionally viewed as being rooted in religion. The substantially enhanced role for Christian education called for by the English Education Act of 1944 was facilitated by "the association of the Christian religion with the cause of democracy . . . ." Basic to the framers of the law was the conviction that "education must have a religious base . . . ." But contrast, Christian education as a school subject in Sweden must, by law, be "objective" and must not propagandize for any particular religion or view of morality— although this is commonly not adhered to in practice. A substantial majority of Swedes accept this "objectivity,"as is indicated by the 1964 study. Given various alternatives on Christian education, the Swedes chose as follows:

□ 25 percent "Christian education should not only give students knowledge but also influence them toward the Christian faith."

□ 66 percent "Christian education should only give students knowledge about religion, but should not attempt to influence them in questions of faith."

□ 4 percent "Any special Christian education is not needed in the schools."

□ 4 percent "None of these agree with my opinion."

□ 1 percent "No answer."

In spite of their relatively low level of church attendance and of orthodox Christian belief, Swedes, as mentioned, are not unfriendly to religion in general. In one 1961 study, asked whether "men in our time need religion," 82 percent of a national sample answered Yes. In 1962 a Swedish magazine sponsored a study of what Swedes regard as important problems. Answers to a question about whether Swedes need a "greater interest in religion" were: 30 percent "very important," 42 percent "quite important," 24 percent "not at all important," 4 percent "can't say."

Nor are most Swedes disturbed by the relation between church and state. In 1957, a national sample of Swedes were asked how they would vote if there were a referendum on the separation of church and state. The results: 18 percent would vote for it, 51 percent would vote against it and 34 percent were undecided.

Yet some pious people, particularly high-church Lutherans, favor such a separation. They argue that the church would be free from government pressures and could become a community of authentic believers. On the other hand, some opinion not sympathetic to the church favors the present relationship precisely because it makes the church subject to some control by the government, the most important being the government's potential power in the appointment of clergy and the control of the budget. An example of this power was seen in the 1950s when the government exerted pressure on the church to allow women to be ordained. High-church opinion bitterly opposed the measure, but with government support it passed the Church Assembly.

Within the church, and outside of it, there are a number of conflicting opinions about the most desirable relationship between state and church and just how this might be realized. Indeed, it has been clear for a number of years that there has been intense disagreement within the church over such issues.

One indication of how favorably the Swedish people regard the church is that the great majority would request church membership if such membership were no longer automatic. A 1958 study of Swedes over 15 found that, if the church were disestablished, 72 percent would join, 19 percent would not join and 9 percent were undecided. In 1961, a sample of Swedes were asked how well they thought the "state churches and the state church clergy were performing their duties." Their verdict was that the churches and clergy were doing tolerably well. Results: 25 percent very well, 53 percent fairly well, 9 percent not especially well, 3 percent poorly and 10 percent can't say.

Comparing the clergy with other occupations, Swedes apparently rank clergymen lower in their usefulness to society than Americans do. Indeed, on this count, Swedes ranked the clergy lower than dentists and business executives. On the other hand, Swedes rank clergymen *higher* in intellectual ability than Americans do. The fact is that the clergy of the state church are graduates of the same prestigious universities as other professionals, and have the status of "akademiker"; whereas the great majority of American clergymen come from little-known denominational institutions. These findings come from a study of American and Swedish university students, who were asked to rank clergymen, and seven other occupational groups, according to usefulness to society, intellectual ability, and prestige. The Swedes and the Americans gave clergymen the same prestige ranking.

The indifference of Swedes toward religion and toward their state church certainly seem clear from all the statistics. But what can be said for the other side of the relationship? How much influence does religion in general, the state church, or the clergy have on the people of Sweden?

It does not take much study of contemporary Sweden to conclude that influence from religious sources is minimal. The church has no illusions about the magnitude of her influence. In fact, the Swedish contributor to a recent symposium sponsored by the World Council of Churches aptly entitled his contribution, "Where the Church No Longer Shapes the Common Life."

The clergy and the church are neutral in political questions. It is almost inconceivable for a clergyman to officially support any political party or position, even though there are fewer sanctions against his participation as a private individual than in many other societies. In recent decades, the church has had little influence on public policy of any kind. It is even difficult for the church to speak out on questions of morality without being subject to a barrage of criticism, particularly when it takes a conservative position.

In 1964, when the bishops deplored the "privatizing" of sexual life and reasserted their 1951 view that premarital intercourse was sinful, they received sharp criticism in a number of Liberal and Social Democratic papers. The headline of a critical editorial in one Stockholm paper was "What do the Bishops Know about Love?"

In Swedish politics, religious beliefs or affiliations are irrelevant—except to the extent that some of the names of the Liberal Party lists are chosen for their free-church affiliations. No religious party has ever been able to elect a representative to the riksdag; the most recent attempt was made by the Christian Democratic Assembly, formed in 1964 and largely supported by Pentacostals and other fundamentalist groups.

Members of the government, or political leaders, virtually never invoke God or any religious sanction in any context. During a television interview in the early 1960s, Gunnar Heckscher, the leader of the Conservative Party from 1961 to 1964, even admitted being an atheist though he claimed to be sympathetic to the Christian tradition. Even though the Conservative Party is the party of those most strongly involved in the Church of Sweden, this surprising admission caused Heckscher no apparent difficulties!

Various studies have shown that Swedes who are religious engage in less premarital sexual behavior than the less religious, and are generally more conservative in their attitudes toward sex. It is also clear that those with a strong involvement in the state church (predominantly the upper and middle classes) tend to support the Conservative Party, while those strongly committed to the free churches (predominantly the middle class and workers) tend to support the Liberal Party or the very small Christian Democratic Assembly.

When it comes to religion, then, it seems that Swedes

behave in much the same manner as a persnickety dinner guest. Swedes are content to accept invitations to the church meal, but after allowing the table to be set and sampling a few hors d'oeuvres, they invariably snub their noses at the entrée.

Perhaps a look into the history of the church in Sweden will give us some insight into this curious situation.

Christianity came late to Sweden. An established Catholic Church had existed there only four centuries before the Reformation of the 16th century. As in England and Denmark, the Reformation in Sweden occurred through the decision of a king, Gustav Vasa (reigned 1523-60). He revolted against the Catholic Church, at least at first, for wholly political and economic reasons. He wanted to create a strong, centralized, and secure nation-state. To do that, he had to reduce the Catholic Church's economic position. In 1527 he gained the consent of the riksdag to reduce the church's land holdings; at his death in 1560, the church's lands had been totally confiscated.

Actually, the first step in the Reformation in Sweden came in 1527 when the riksdag proclaimed that the word of God should "be preached pure"—a step that supported Lutheran doctrine, but was not strong enough to disturb non-Lutherans. The new law emphasized the authority of scripture over the Church. In 1536, a Church Assembly helped the Reformation in a number of ways: It made the Swedish mass and manual obligatory throughout Sweden, and it gave the clergy the right to marry. An autonomous national church had in fact appeared, and orthodoxy was officially established in 1544.

The desire for orthodoxy dominated Swedish religious and political thought until the eighteenth century, and remained a powerful force until after the mid-nineteenth century. Vestiges of it continued up to the Religious Freedom Law of 1951, which dispensed with the rule that all cabinet ministers and civil servants had to be members of the Church of Sweden. For the population in general, this law made it possible to leave the Swedish church without having to enter another religious congregation.

In 1634, the concept of the religious unity of the state— that the state and the church were one and the same—was first incorporated in the Swedish Constitution. This concept was reaffirmed in all successive Constitutions, including the most recent one that was adopted in 1809. This is in striking contrast to England and Holland, where tolerance toward other Christians began to develop in the seventeenth century.

Just as the seventeenth century marks the establishment of religious orthodoxy in Sweden, so the eighteenth century marks its decline. Two forces contributed to the breakdown of this orthodoxy. One was the skepticism and rationalism of the Enlightenment. The other, interesting enough, was almost the opposite. It was a movement called pietism, which originated in Germany in the seventeenth century and later spread to Sweden. Pietism was essentially a reaction to formalism and intellectualism, and it stressed the need for Bible study and personal religious experience.

Pietists in Sweden quickly became the targets of much repressive legislation. The most far-reaching was a government edict of 1726, which forbade any assembly for worship, public or private, without the presence of a parish clergyman. (The exception: private prayers.) The penalties for violation were fines, imprisonment, or banishment from the country. This law infringing as it did on religious activities, prompted many Swedes, including non-Pietists, to become hostile to the established church. The law was even criticized from within the church.

The Enlightenment contributed to the breakdown of orthodoxy by influencing the church to become more rational and quite secular. Gustav III, who attained the throne after a coup d'état in 1771, was a full-fledged Enlightenment king. In 1781 he gave foreign Christians the right to form their own congregations, to build their own churches, and to have their children trained by their own clergy. The next year similar rights were given to Jews. For the remaining Swedes, however, the compulsions to attend church and take communion remained intact, as did other rules governing religious activity.

Meanwhile, a great deal of freedom was growing within the church itself. By Calvinist standards, there was an absence of puritanism and narrow moralistic concerns. The clergy was well educated, and placed a good deal of value on scholarship. The better-educated among them led upper-class styles of life. Many tilled their own farms, and made contributions to agricultural science. Traditionally, the clergy functioned as teachers, doctors, and parish politicians, and even took care to the population registers, in effect acting as Anglo-American county clerks—a function they have carried down to the present. With all of their activities, it is not surprising that to many of them the care of souls was of quite secondary importance.

At the higher levels, the Swedish church had become very much secularized by the first half of the nineteenth century. Thus, becoming a bishop was considered a natural niche for leading cultural figures, regardless of their religious beliefs or training in theology. Esaias Tegnér, a professor and poet of the time, upon his appointment as a bishop, wrote to a friend that "A pagan I am and shall remain."

Partly as a reaction to such secularization, the church began returning to a greater orthodoxy and social conservatism in the 1840s. Up to the middle of the 1880s and—to some extent—even later, the church held reactionary ideologies that rationalized and defended the existing benevolent and hierarchial order against liberalism at first, and against socialism later. Two or three decades of internal conflict ensued, during which the church provided the major support for the values of traditional Swedish society. The already hostile views of the Social Democrats, and some of the Liberals, toward the church and religion were therefore further aggravated. Thus, while modern notions of religious freedom and tolerance, equality and popular democracy were sweeping Western Europe in the nineteenth century, the Swedish church was defending the old order. The fact that the church so completely committed itself to reactionary values during this period is crucial to understanding the secularization of the working class and the educated middle class.

It was not until the first decade of the twentieth century that a rapprochement began between the church and the Social Democrats and other popular movements—the union, the free churches, and the temperance societies. But it may already have been too late for the church to expect to ever again exert a powerful influence over the Swedish people.

Our review of Swedish religious history has shown the changes that have taken place in the relationship between the church and the common people. But what is the official relationship of the church and the state?

Since the 1809 constitution that reaffirmed their union, relations between the church and state have been marked by three major developments.

☐ the legal development of religious freedom.

☐ the institution of a Church Assembly to replace the riksdag in dealing with matters of internal concern to the church.

☐ the transfer of a number of the church's educational and political duties to the civil community.

A proposal to allow church members to resign was first introduced into the riksdag in 1824. In 1860, a modified version of this proposal was approved. It was not until nearly a century later, however, with the passage of the Religious Freedom Law in 1951, that it became possible for someone to leave the church without entering another religious congregation. Yet up to the mid 1960s only about 40,000 Swedes left the church.

In the parliamentary reforms of 1866, the clergy lost formal representation in the riksdag. In exchange, the riksdag established a Church Assembly with the authority to veto government decisions regarding church law and the prerogatives of the clergy. At the same time, the riksdag gave the church and clergy greater authority over still more of their internal affairs. In 1949 the Church Assembly, for the first time, came to consist of a majority of laymen. Today, the Swedish church has more autonomy from the government than does the state church in either Norway or Denmark—but not so much as in Finland.

Over the years, the distinction between ecclesiastical and civil authority has been sharpened. Legislation passed in 1862 took away many of the secular functions of the church and clergy and gave them to the civil community. Subsequent legislation has removed the clergy's duties in social welfare and education, including teaching religion in the schools.

In sum, the great amount of secularism in Sweden can perhaps be explained in the following way:

Religion has never become a major source of cleavage among Swedes. This is contrary to the situation in the United States, England, and the Netherlands, where a religious diversity has thrived. Such differences seem to stimulate religious concerns.

As mentioned, during the crucial period of early modernization—particularly during the last two decades of the nineteenth century—the church solidly aligned itself with the old order and its traditional values. State Church Lutheranism, with its emphasis on absolute doctrinal authority and its essentially medieval view of society, was inherently less receptive to egalitarianism and tolerance than Calvinism and the more individualistic forms of Protestantism. This alienated the growing segments of society oriented toward modern values as it did elsewhere in Europe, but the division was particularly sharp in Sweden.

Sweden had a relatively late but extraordinarily successful modernization. With modernization came a new respect for science and empiricism, which thoroughly discredited nineteenth century society, with its traditional and idealistic values. The dominant values of contemporary Sweden support agnosticism and nonbelief rather than traitional religion, pragmatism rather than conventional morality.

December 1968

FURTHER READING:

The New Sweden by Frederic Fleisher (New York: David McKay, 1967). This is the most recent and perhaps the best popular account of modern Sweden in English.

The Public Dialogue in Sweden: Current Issues of Social, Esthetic and Moral Debate translated by Claude Stephenson (Stockholm: P.A. Norstedt, 1964), contains an excellent overview of the public debate in Sweden "in the vacuum after Christianity" by a leading young Swedish intellectual.

Sweden: Prototype of Modern Society by Richard F. Tomasson (New York: Random House, 1970) contains a more detailed account of the religious situation in Sweden.

The Future of the Islamic Religion

GUENTHER LEWY

The history of Islam begins in Arabia with Mohammed's move from Mecca to Medina in the year 622 of the
Christian era. Within less than a century the Arabs had
swept through North Africa into Spain and France and
had reached the banks of the Indus River. A great new
civilization had been born.

Today there are about 350,000,000 Muslims in the
world—embracing one-seventh of the earth's population.
Modern Islam presents a wide spectrum of religious and
political ideology, ranging from the ultra-orthodox to the
modernistic-secularistic. It is a not-to-be-ignored factor in
the politics of the Near East and North Africa, as well as
in Pakistan and Indonesia. In these pages I want to discuss
the Muslim religion as a political force in the history of the
Islamic states, and to venture some comments about the
future of Islam in the modern world.

There are two important themes in the history of the
Islamic states. The major theme is submission to political

authority. The minor theme is rebellion against an unjust ruler. Both themes spring directly from the teachings of the Muslim religion.

When Mohammed organized his followers into a permanent community, it existed in order to perpetuate the new religion. This first community was a theocracy, at once religious and political. God and His revealed law were the supreme authority; Mohammed, His apostle, was the Lord's viceregent on earth.

When the prophet died in A.D. 632, the community elected Abu-Bekr, Mohammed's faithful friend, as their new leader. He was called the successor (caliph) of the Prophet. His political power was as complete as that of Mohammed. The first caliph nominated his successor, Omar, and the Arabian community of Medina accepted and confirmed this nomination. The third and fourth caliphs were also elected, but violence had begun playing a considerable role in the succession. Of the four caliphs following Mohammed, only the first died a natural death; the other three were murdered.

The fifth caliph nominated his son as his successor, thus founding a dynasty (the Umayyads) and formally introducing the hereditary principle. This precedent was followed for the next 400 years. By the time the Abbasid dynasty in Baghdad replaced the Umayyads in the year 750, hereditary autocratic rule had become firmly established, a practice leaning heavily upon the ancient Persian concept of kingship by divine right. Whereas early tradition had considered the caliphate an elective office, the traditional number of electors now was reduced to one, a change that amounted to an implicit acceptance of the hereditary principle: The predecessor appointed his successor. But the myth of election continued to exist, drawing strength from the oath of allegiance paid to the new prince in the capital and throughout the growing Islamic empire.

Islamic constitutional doctrine developed, during the first two centuries of Islam, as a rationalization of the existing practice. The doctrine involved a kind of social contract. It held that the ultimate source of political authority was God, who had provided for a ruler to command the people and thus ensure peace and protect the faithful. By accepting this office, the caliph promised to exercise his powers within the limits of the law. He confirmed this promise in a contract (bay'a)with the representatives of the community. If he violated this contract, the people were absolved of allegiance and could elect another ruler.

The doctrine of a contract between ruler and ruled made no provision, short of complete revolution, for removing a bad caliph. So if the doctrine were to serve the interests of the ruling class, it needed modification; it had to be stated in ways that stressed the duty of obedience, rather than the right to rebel. The occasional religious saying affirming the duty of Muslims to rebel against a ruler was checked—by the deliberate introduction of far more numerous sayings that branded the creation of disorder without adequate justification a mortal sin. All earthly authority was seen as ordained by God, and if a tyrant ruled he was simply God's punishment for man's sin.

The enormous Arab empire that the first caliphs had built did not last. Even the caliphate was swept aside by anyone who could take and keep power in the many smaller Arab states that succeeded the empire.

Adjusting theory to current reality (a pattern throughout Islamic history), the religious teachers now held that anyone in effective possession of power had to be obeyed—no matter how he had acquired power or how impious or barbaric his conduct. The Islamic community was intact, it was argued, as long as the secular government recognized the Koran and the traditions of Mohammed; consulted the religious teachers; and created conditions so that individual Muslims could obey the holy law. For centuries thereafter, the dominant theme of the Muslim countries was political quietism, supported and encouraged by religious arguments.

But the minor theme of rebellion against sinful leaders never died out. Thus members of the Khawarij sect viewed themselves as saints under a moral obligation to revolt against sinful government and its supporters. Under the Umayyad caliphs, these "Puritans of Islam" spread terror among their opponents, often killing male Muslims along with women and children. And the Shi'ite Muslims, of non-Arabic descent, pressed for an order in which all Muslims would be equal and Arab birth would not carry special privileges.

Indeed, throughout the first 1100 years of its existence, Islamic political life had its share of rebellions. The orthodox doctrine stressing the duty of obedience was always beset by heresies and sects that taught the duty of revolt against impious or oppressive authority. These seemingly contradictory doctrines are, of course, related. Muslim political theories and political institutions failed to assure a peaceful resolution of social and economic issues; they did not provide for an orderly succession of rulers. Regional and tribal loyalties remained strong. In this situation, rebellions and military mutinies were frequent. In Algiers, for example, between 1671 and 1818 some 14 of the 30 rulers achieved power through a military rebellion or by assassinating their predecessors. These rivalries, internal wars, and rebellions signaled the failure of Islamic political institutions—and at the same time ensured the survival of Islam itself. The rebellions, often inspired by religious motives, acted as a safety valve that helped renovate political authority even as it attacked a particular ruler.

The centuries-long tradition of autocratic rule and political quietism, interrupted from time to time by futile rebellions, lasted in the Islamic world until the French Revolution. The new slogans of liberty, equality, and popular sovereignty were easy to accept because they were expressed in non-Christian terms: Carried by European soldiers and traders into the Middle East, these slogans breached the walls of that ancient citadel of autocracy. Almost immediately began the Westernization that is still in progress more than 170 years later, and that has created the turbulence that can be observed today throughout the Islamic world, from North Africa to Pakistan and Indonesia.

Islamic intellectuals reacted to this new reality in different ways. If we take an overall view of the last 100 years, we can distinguish four main groups:

—MODERNISTS—who aim at integrating Western democracy into a rejuvenated Islam;

—TRADITIONALISTS—religious teachers for the most part, who see no need for basic doctrinal change and are willing to go along with any existing form of government;

—FUNDAMENTALISTS—who want to return to the theocratic foundation of early Islam; and

—SECULAR NATIONALISTS—who may still appeal to the Islamic emotions of the masses but who seek modernization and a new secular foundation for the legitimacy of government.

The modernists, many of them Western-educated, argue that Islam and democracy are compatible. They point to the *bay'a,* the ancient doctrine of a contract between the ruler and the ruled, and they make much of the Prophet's having consulted important members of the aristocracy of Medina.

But this attempt to plant modern political ideals in the Islamic tradition is based on a failure to understand both democracy and Islam completely. The political practices of a tribal society do *not* fit the complexities of the 20th century. The democratic idea of elected, representative bodies legislating in spiritual matters offends the very basis of Islam. This attempt to reconcile democracy and Islam, to be sure, has served the need of some Muslim intellectuals to restate their faith in terms of the fashionable ideology of the day, and it has fostered pride in the Muslim past. It has not, however, provided guidance in solving the political problems of modern nation-building.

The traditionalists have been the least perturbed by the political and intellectual challenge of the West. Most of the religious teachers, the *ulama,* have cooperated with the newest Arab nation-states and with their secular rulers. They have adjusted themselves to the powerful currents of nationalism, even though orthodox Islam recognizes neither geographical nor ethnic boundaries. In Egypt, the ulama even condemned the Muslim Brotherhood because it used force in opposing the secular government of Naguib and Nasser. The ulama of Pakistan have gracefully accepted the country's failure to achieve an Islamic constitution, although they and their allies had worked for one for many years. The prestige of the ulama, especially in the rural areas, is still high, but they have almost no influence on the thinking of those elite groups that hold the reins of government.

The third type of response to the revolutionary impact of Western thinking has been fundamentalism. Most recently fundamentalism has been expressed in the movement of the Muslim Brotherhood, an organization founded in 1928 by an Egyptian elementary-school teacher. The Brotherhood wants the establishment of an Islamic state, governed if possible by a caliph, which will carry out the rules and injunctions of the Koran and the tradition. Adultery, usury, drinking, and gambling will be vigorously suppressed; marriage and the begetting of children will be encouraged. The Brotherhood regards narrow nationalism as a "hideous pestilence"; it advocates, instead, the union of all Islamic countries and the driving out of any European influences through a holy war. The Brotherhood also seeks the eventual conquest and conversion of all the rest of the world. The legitimacy of secular governments that neglect the teachings of Islam is denied by the Brotherhood, which exhorts its followers to fight such governments by all available means.

The fourth category of contemporary Islamic political thought is secular nationalism, which rejects religion as a basis for political action. The secular nationalist view was propounded in 1950 by Khalid Muhammad Khalid. Openly acknowledging his intellectual debt to Voltaire, Rousseau, and Thomas Paine, Khalid called the Islamic priesthood a reactionary, totalitarian body that had dragged the people into "an abyss of servility and subjection." Theocratic government, whether in Christianity or Islam, had always been the worst possible type of tyranny, Khalid insistd.

Khalid's ideas are very similar to the theoretical basis of Egypt's politics under Naguib and Nasser. The officers who overthrew the monarchy in 1952, General Naguib has said, did not want to turn their backs on the Islamic faith. But they felt that the messages preached by the Prophet had to be interpreted in the light of the great changes since those early days. "There is nothing in the Koran," Naguib has written, "that calls for theocratic government." President Nasser's allusions to Islam are primarily a matter of foreign policy, and not ideology. The basis of Nasser's claim to legitimacy is secular.

In the years since World War II, Islam—which had been waning as a political force before the war—seemed to revive. Confidence in the West was shaken by the war, which seemed to have brought Western democracy to the brink of destruction. The increased political pressure of the Western powers, the presence of foreign troops, and finally the creation of Israel all increased nationalist sentiment.

Since the masses were still predominantly Muslim, and since the nationalist leaders sought to mobilize these masses, nationalism was increasingly tied to religion. In the Near East, Islam was described as the product of the Arab national genius. On the Indian subcontinent, Islam saw a powerful resurgence through the creation of Pakistan. The hold of religion on the Muslim masses has, of course, benefited the cause of fundamentalist extremism. By the end of World War II, the Muslim Brotherhood had at least a million followers in Egypt and several other Near Eastern countries, and—despite harassment and repression—the movement continues to show strength.

Now that the old value system is crumbling under the impact of technology and mass communications, fundamentalism seems to offer salvation and meaning in life by striving to resurrect an idealized past. The submerged masses still have no stake in the modern world and are disappointed by the failure of the new governments to bring a real improvement in their lot. To them, a militant, messianic radicalism glorifying passion and struggle has considerable appeal. Since 1945, several secular nationalist leaders in Egypt, Iran, and Pakistan have been assassinated by fundamentalist extremists; in 1965, a plot against President Nasser was uncovered and his assassination foiled. Clearly, even though Islam is often expressed merely as ritual, it is still a force to be reckoned with.

Yet it is doubtful that fundamentalism and other forms of neo-orthodoxy truly have a future. The forces of secularization increasingly undermine religion. Urbanization and industrialization break up tribal life and weaken the traditional family. The state almost everywhere is in the hands of secular nationalists, who may still use traditional symbols and an Islamic vocabulary, but who increasingly adhere to a secular path. Religious leaders, unable to confront the problems of a country challenged by Western technology and power, ever more lose their prestige and influence to the new secular leadership. Islam is neither persecuted nor abolished; it is simply being bypassed as no longer relevant.

The struggle for independence from the colonial powers weakened political authority and the legitimacy of the state. At that time, the task of the patriot was to defy the alien state and subvert it. Today the most urgent job is to reverse this trend, to build political cohesion and a stable government that can deal with the problems of nation-building and social change, as well as to find a new basis for legitimacy. The constitutions of most Islamic countries still provide that Islam be the religion of the state and that the head of state be a Muslim, but such provisions are of largely deferential character. They cannot guarantee national integration or legitimize political power. Sovereignty can no longer be derived from religious tradition. To be considered legitimate, political authority must confront the problems created by the uprooting of the old structure of society.

Many governments in today's Islamic world quite consciously stress the tie between modernization and legitimacy. At the same time they often dismiss the Western democratic idea of rival parties competing for the allegiance of the voters as unsuitable for regimes struggling to accomplish rapid social change. An Egyptian, writing about Nasser's Arab Socialist Union (the regime's official agent for mobilizing mass support), stressed that this movement was not an ordinary political party but represented the whole people. "The people," he continued, "are not limited by partisan principles but are gathered together around their national goals to achieve the mission of Arab nationalism and to stimulate their efforts for the sound political, social, and economic construction of the nation." Strong-man regimes like those of Nasser, or Ayub Kyan of Pakistan, are facilitated by the traditional subordination of the individual to the state or community in Muslim political practice, and by the Islamic respect for power.

Still, power and force alone are not enough to inspire loyalty. Hence the appeal to nationalism, social reform, and modernization, accompanied by a religious ceremonial in order to bolster legitimacy. Islam has been quite adaptive in the past and it may well adjust itself to this new situation as well. It may in time become what much of Christianity has already become: A body of private religious beliefs, fulfilling the psychological needs of some individuals and contributing to a sense of national heritage, but without practical implication for the conduct of the state. Though such a kind of Islam may be radically different from anything history has known so far, it would be presumptuous to maintain that such a religion should no longer be called Islamic.

March 1968

FURTHER READING:

The Caliphate by Thomas W. Arnold (New York: Barnes and Noble, 1966, revised edition). The classic study of the institution of the caliphate—written in 1924 and brought up to date by Sylvia G. Haim, a leading authority on the history of ideas in the Arab world.

Mohammedanism: An Historical Survey by Hamilton A. R. Gibb (New York: Oxford University Press, Galaxy Books, 1962, second revised edition). The best brief general introduction to Islam and its contemporary situation, written by the present dean of Islamic studies.

The Politics of Social Change in the Middle East and North Africa by Manfred Halpern (Princeton, N.J.: Princeton University Press, 1963). A sophisticated analysis of the political ramifications of modernization in the major centers of the Islamic world.

Nationalism and Revolution in the Arab World by Sharabi Hisham (Princeton, N.J.: D. van Nostrand, 1966). A concise overview of recent political developments in the Arab world, together with documentary materials illustrating the author's discussion of political ideology, constitutional structures, and coups d'etat.

Challenge to Catholicism in Latin America

Religious elites and professional holy men hold a more distinctive place in history than warriors or kings. As the guardians of spiritual values and moral authority, they may emerge as the centers of ideological ferment in periods of social crisis and transformation. Such is the situation in Latin America.

Latin American religious elites are composed of the varying complexes of leadership within the Roman Catholic church. This leadership is not confined simply to those occupying the top statuses in the religious system; a person belongs in the religious elite if, as an individual or group member, he is able to exert a decisive influence on the development of the Catholic system or the wider social order. This influence may be tradition-oriented, innovative, or simply neutralizing.

Elitism in Latin America must be viewed within its historical context, within the institutional framework which gives it social meaning. In the case of Latin American

Catholicism this framework is the church in relation to its history and thus to its evolving connections with the social structure. It sets the context for developments within the church, and for the developing impact of the church on the social situation. To know what the Roman Catholic church is today in Latin America and what internal and external lines of change it is taking, it is necessary to know what it *was*—where it stood in the traditional social order. Four major patterns of the traditional church emerge.

FORMAL VS. FOLK RELIGION. During the seventeenth century a deep cleavage began to develop between the formal church and the "Catholic" religion. Because of a shortage of clergy, the hierarchy's fusion with the ruling classes, and the missionaries' "in-name-only" conception of Christian conversion, a major part of the religious needs of the masses came to be satisfied through extrasacramental practices, private devotions, worship of patron saints, and participation in festive religious-social activities. This gap between ecclesia and religious needs became institutionalized. Although the church as a formal body was to be found in the cathedrals and chapels, Catholicism became grounded in nonecclesiastical social units—in the family, in brotherhoods, in the community, and in the informal contacts of the everyday world. The priest and his sacramental authority tended to be peripheral to man's quest for salvation.

ORGANIZATIONAL WEAKNESS. The Latin American church, and policy-making organization, emerged as a series of isolated ecclesiastical units, each one focused almost exclusively uncoordinated in its regional and diocesan activities, and structurally awkward; lines of communication and authority were weak and confused. Since routine administration and ad hoc problem-solving outweighed planning and programming, the church's activities were not oriented to a set of central and shared religious goals or autonomous, long-range policies. Because the church was hierarchically undeveloped, internally divided, and relatively incapable of using its canonical structure as an effective system of command and action, its elite groups were not able to take a clear and unified position as *religious* leaders.

SECULAR CONTROL. Traditional Catholic elites have been subjected to secular control over most of the past 450 years. The Spanish crown exercised close control over the church in the New World, and as a result the hierarchy had to work through secular elites in order to survive and initiate religious activities of every sort. In this situation the clergy's energies were consumed in short-run political maneuvering and in creating viable coalitions with other power groups. Religious elites were prepared to maximize their position when secular conditions were favorable, to exercise restraint in periods of uncertainty, and to be inconsistent if the situation demanded it.

MORAL CONFUSION. Because they lacked a unified vision of the church's mission and were subjected to inconstant secular domination, Catholic elites failed to create and institutionalize a religious and moral foundation for the growth of a common system of societal values. Their potential capacity to symbolize and require conformity to a higher moral order was never realized. Instead of functioning as creators of a religiously based value system and as impartial leaders in the moral realm, the Catholic elites actually fomented moral confusion. Consequently an enduring association between secular political strength and moral legitimacy was established, and politics became an arena in which a "religious" battle over ends, rather than a competition over who is best qualified to lead, took place. There is little doubt that this early link between secular power and moral authority has helped to create the political turmoil characteristic of contemporary Latin America.

Thus, the church's achievement of influence and social control did not depend on its capacities as a Christian religious system. In the main, the church and its leaders drew their importance from alliances with secular powers and from their multiple involvements in education, social welfare, and adminstration. The scope of the church's functions was very wide, but each function was dependent on the maintenance of the status quo. For this reason, the church continued to align itself with the conservative factions of Latin American society as a major survival strategy until the beginning of the twentieth century.

Until the turn of the century Catholicism held a dual monopoly as the official national religion of many Latin American republics and as the universal religious culture. But the rise of secular political movements of the left and of salvation-oriented Protestant sects has broken this monopoly. Both movements offer a new reward system, assume a militant posture against the existing social order, and articulate a cohesive set of anti-Catholic values. By competing with Catholicism at the value level they have forced it to assume the guise of an ideology for conservative groups rather than a major cultural system. In addition, the new movements provide their adherents with a program of social action to be carried out in lay organizations which combine enthusiasm with group responsibility at the grass-roots level. Even the novice layman has a definite status, a meaningful set of responsibilities to be carried out.

The traditional Catholic system is ill equipped to counter such militant sects. For more than four centuries it has made no attempt to utilize the layman as a religious system resource or even to integrate him meaningfully into the system. Since the entire Catholic system was entwined with the institutions of the total society, there was no real need to utilize the layman as an instrument of religious influence. Why organize the grass roots to "win the neighbor"? All the neighbors were baptized Catholics, as were the people of the next village, *patrones* and slaves, peasants and military officers. Moreover, the hierarchical divisions within the church and within the laity provided no basis for integration, whereas the Communists and Socialists, as well as the Pentecostal sects, stress horizontal solidarity and communality, both ideologically and structurally. Such slogans as "From each according to his ability; to each according to his needs," and "We are all brothers in Christ; no priests, no servants, no rich, no poor," provide a feeling of solidarity which is closely related to existing kinship and community ties and with which Catholicism cannot compete, even on religious grounds.

During the twentieth century, the traditional church in one Latin American country after another has discovered that its capacity for influence has been severely weakened, not only by the nineteenth century anticlerical legislation, but also by a series of subtle sociological trends: the growth of an urban social class, internal population shifts, the strengthening of technical and scientific centers in secular universities, and the emergence of many competing interest groups. These trends have tended to weaken or obscure traditional lines of influence and sources of status. In addition to these broad patterns of change, specific trends on the local, national, and international levels have rendered traditional Catholicism's position of influence especially tenuous.

There is a characteristic tendency for a modern, nationally focused society to move and adapt as a total system. As the Latin American countries develop economically and politically, the growth of institutional interdependence brings all specialized functional units together into a more integrated whole such that the primary integrative level is found at the level of the total society. National, rather than regional or local, events and institutions dominate the rhythm of social life. This means that special interests, including influence-oriented religious groups, require clearcut national strategies and forceful national organizations if they are to make an impact on society. An ambitious religious system must fulfill several organizational tasks: Religious impact must be developed to cope with the total society's trends, rhythms, and problems; religious action must depend on generated, rather than "gathered," loyalty and must be consciously planned and coordinated; and religious programs must have both a long-term goal and a short-range adaptability to specialized local circumstances.

Traditional Catholicism is not integrated at the national level and therefore not prepared to cope with the new rhythm of social life. It is given to localized, ad hoc problem-solving, situational alliances, and a short-run goal perspective. It is thus extremely handicapped in the face of national institutional integration.

The Latin American church is under heavy pressure from various hierarchies of international Catholicism to resolve its problems and "put its house in order." Both the Holy See and various national episcopal conferences in France, Belgium, Germany, Canada, and the United States are concerned over the Latin American church, for it not only encompasses more than one-third of the church's total baptized membership, but also appears to be impotant in the face of Communist expansion among the masses. Moreover, the Second Vatican Council dealt quite plainly with issues, policies, and innovations bearing directly on the problems of traditional Latin American Catholicism, and the Latin American church is thus considered a key "test site" for the conciliar reforms and for the future of Catholicism in general.

Under the foregoing pressures to maintain and regain an influential position in a changing society, Catholic leaders in Latin America are desperately seeking new mechanisms to strengthen the church's spiritual life and provide it with new bases of influence in the wider institutional order. Although there are still major internal divisions and much disagreement over goals, certain patterns are emerging with respect to the church's internal organization and to its links with society.

Considerable energy and leadership in the Latin American church are being diverted to the task of making the church relevant and effective in the modern situation. The most noticeable change which has occurred is centralization, the establishment of tighter lines of authority and communication within the hierarchies, and the enlargement of the de facto powers of national and continental episcopal councils. The traditional isolation and autonomy of bishops and local level clergy has been reduced in favor of coordinated activities and policies oriented toward the church as a whole.

Another theme of elite activity is the creation of a socially relevant Catholic ideology, drawn largely from the social encyclicals and new theologies which have been produced in the church over the last 75 years. Leo XIII's *Rerum Novarum* (1891), Pius XI's *Quadragesimo Anno* (1961) are frequently quoted documents, and the names of Maritain, Congar, Rahner, Teilhard de Chardin, Kung, Suenens, and de Lubac—all Europeans—are frequently heard in the socially progressive sectors of the church. Perhaps the greatest source of ideological support for the agents of change within the church has been the ideas and proposals produced by Vatican II, which have given the liberal sectors of Catholicism so much popular reinforcement that those who earlier hesitated to act are gaining new confidence. In Latin America the Catholic liberals have fashioned a powerful and appealing ideology calling for social justice for the deprived, fundamental institutional reforms, social action in the world as a key means of Christian influence, and a concern for man and the human community.

To realize this ideology and to meet the pressing demands of the modern situation, Catholic leaders are attempting to mobilize a new lay missionary force or lay apostolate. Laymen are organized into priest-led cells or associations, in which they are educated and persuaded to infuse their daily relationships with Christian principles. Thus the usually passive layman is to promote Catholicism in his routine activities as worker, friend, club member, or family member in order to re-Christianize the dormant masses, and regain a prominent place in society for the church.

Clusters of elite activity have also differentiated around the political and cultural priorities of the church—that is, its strategy of survival and its role in social change. Four types of elite development can be identified. The first is the traditional base from which the others have differentiated, and three are "new" types.

□ Traditional Catholic elites in Latin America are oriented to the power structure of secular society. Because they feel that the church's interlocking connections with the polity and its manipulation of secular power groups are essential to its survival, these traditional elite members may be called the *politicians*. They look to secular groups for support, protection, and legitimation, and they see the church as a structure of formal, hierarchical positions from which they receive status which is useful in the wider community. They ignore the laity, carry out rituals pro forma, make the sacraments available to those who can pay the fee, and define social evils as implicit in the human situation. Secure in their positions, the traditional elites strongly resist and even satirize the innovations of Vatican II bearing on changes in the liturgy and lay involvement.

□ Of the three new elites, the *papists* (not meant with any opprobrium) stand for a militant, modern Catholicism oriented toward re-Christianizing the world. They reject traditional sources of political involvement in favor of creating a church which relies on its own authority and resources to achieve visibility and influence. These resources are seen as the church structure, social action, and the sacraments. The hierarchy, the clergy, and the laity constitute a missionary elite concerned with expanding the frontiers of Catholic values under the aegis of a hierarchy which extends beyond the local or national level to Rome. Religious action is defined according to traditional Catholic premises on the nature of the church, the validity of its dogmas, and its monopoly of religious charisma.

This militant, apostolic conception of modern Catholicism's relation to society is drawn from developments in the European situation over the past two generations. The most decisive expression of the new mission emerged during the pontificate of Pius XI, and was adopted, with some modifications during the mid-1930s in areas of the Latin American church, where it was expressed in terms of youth programs, apostolic units, and episcopally directed strategies. Although actual successes have been minimal, often because they provoked latent anticlericism, the papists remain a major elite cluster in Latin America, especially Colombia, Argentina, and Mexico.

□ The *pastors* are a small but growing group of bishops and clergy who see their main task as that of building up strong, worship-centered congregations. They seek a formula for effectively welding the priest, the laity, and the sacraments into a single spiritual body. Among the changes the pastors propose are: elaboration of the priest's role from that of isolated ritual leader to include preaching, counseling, and mingling with the laity; involvement of the laity in the liturgy; alteration of parish boundaries to create smaller, more homogeneous congregations; and design of church buildings that reduces the physical distance between priest and worshippers. The vocabulary of the pastors is studded with such terms as cooperation, community, communication, pastoral care, and the meaning of the sacraments—clear indicators of their concern over the quality of religious life.

□ The third new elite group, the *pluralists,* are a rather mixed group whose central premise is that Catholicism in Latin America is but one faith among many others, both secular and religious, and that the church therefore ought to assist in the institutionalization of social justice where-ever possible. They are more concerned with grassroots action than with political alliances, hierachy and clerical-ism, or worship and the sacraments; the essential religious task is that of furthering economic development and social integration.

The pluralists pay special attention to the problems of the poor and the exploited, and they are not averse to co-operative undertakings with other faiths in order to benefit the disadvantaged. Their planning is long-range and societal in scope, since they feel that the church must, as a differentiated agency of moral and social influence, play a positive role in the social revolution occurring in Latin America. And they tend to be highly critical of the other elite groups' methods and orientations as inadequate and misguided. They refer to the conforming, clerical Catholic Action elite as "sacristans" or "goon squads." They talk with bitterness about the traditional "politicos" and their maneuverings. The pastors' exclusive concern with the church's inner life is criticized as "escapism," "retreatism," and "withdrawal."

The foregoing elite groups do not exhaust the kinds of religious elite differentiation to be found in contemporary Latin American Catholicism, but they differ along two major analytical dimensions: the sphere from which they feel the church should gain its influence—either from its internal resources (organization and ritual) or from its external involvement with secular groups and events—and the organizing principle which they feel should structure religious-social relationships. These dimensions can be utilized to construct the following typology:

Structural principle of Catholic activity

		HIERARCHICAL	COOPERATIVE
Sphere from which church influence is to be drawn	EXTERNAL	Politicians	Pluralists
	INTERNAL	Pastors	Papists

Two patterns are clear with respect to the conditions of the "new" elites' emergence. First, the strength of the politicians in the national hierarch is directly related to the number of remaining church-state links; where these ties are numerous, the politicians' survival strategies are viable, and they in turn tend to limit the growth of the papists and the pastors. But pluralist counterelites develop as a reaction against the political posture and conservatism of the politicians. Although the papists and the pastors cannot undertake the upgrading or restructuring of church organization and life because the church is neither autonomous nor, at this point, in need of it, the pluralists are able to counter the politicians in the sphere of secular action and thereby flourish.

On the other hand, the papists appear to play a key facilitating role in the development of the other two new elites, pastors and pluralists. With their emphasis on political detachment, improving church organization, involving laymen, and on defining an articulated set of theological conceptions of "mission in society," the papists form a bridge between the traditional politicans and the new pastors and pluralists. Institutional change in Roman Catholicism requires the imprimatur of the hierachy, and the papists provide for a structural reorganization which makes the granting of this imprimatur to the efforts of the pluralists and pastors much more likely. Once the church has undergone a series of structural and ideological changes, including a "liberalization" of the hierachy, the pluralist and pastoral strategies become a fully integrated part of a total mission and thus may add strength to the church and aid in the positive development of society.

It may be possible for the pastors and pluralists to form a working alliance if they can manage to utilize the organizational capacities of the papists without having to accept their parallel emphases on authoritarianism, monopolism, and ultramontanism. Unless the two more radical groups recognize the importance of centralized coordination and integration, they run the risk of dispersion and thus defeat. They actually have a long-range advantage in that there are certain well-developed trends in Latin America toward sociological pluralism and increased religious competition, factors which will require the church to forego some of its rigidity and emphasis on ritual and organizational uniformity in favor of the changes proposed by the pastors and pluralists if it is to retain its influence. The institutional dilemma, of course, is how to achieve the advantages of "denominationalism"—internal religious, ritual, and ideological differentiation—without falling into the pattern of fragmentation which characterizes the Protestant tradition.

We hear a great deal in the church today about *aggiornamento* or "bringing the church up to date." From these phrases and the ideas that accompany them, the observer tends to see the whole dynamic of the church's development in terms of the struggle between the "conservatives" and the "liberals." But within the present typological distinctions, it is possible to clarify the crucial distinction between "bringing the church up to date" or "renewal" and "reform" of the Catholic system. Many Catholic leaders and laymen champion Pope John XXIII as the most advanced spokesman of the "liberal" camp. But this is a mistake. His major emphasis was on renewal—on raising the internal effectiveness of the church's structure and adjusting traditional ideas to the modern times. He was not bent on making deep structural changes in the church—such as those taken seriously by the pastors and the pluralists. To renew is not to reform. Consequently, one of the most critical tasks of the new Catholic elites is how to secure basic structural changes that bear decisively on the special religious problems and social issues in Latin America. The "happy days" of John XXIII created a phase of risky optimism that has already suffered some deep shocks.

The strength of the four elites varies from country to country. Columbia, Argentina, and Peru are strongholds of the politicians, and, as expected, there are also pluralist religious groups in these countries. The papists are also strong in Argentina and Coloumbia, as well as in Mexico. Brazil, Venezuela, and Chile, on the other hand, are the main centers of pastor-pluralist developments, and strong pastoral emphases are to be found in certain regions of Bolivia and Guatemala.

The broad comparative picture suggests two generalizations. First, elite developments in Chilean and Brazilian Catholicism appear to be on the threshold of a new phase, having partially broken the political tradition and, in turn, moved through a modified papist period. Thus, in these countries, as in certain Venezuelan and Argentinian dioceses, an institutional basis for effective pastoral and pluralist developments exists to a limited degree. Second, the pastoral and pluralist elites gain in importance as Christian Democratic parties emerge within the national political system. These Catholic-oriented political movements serve to absorb political-type strategies within the church, thus allowing pluralists and pastors to concentrate on religious values and religious action. Moreover, they provide an institutionalized means for the papists to link political action with Catholic values without formally involving the church in politics.

Within the total context of Latin American development, each of the new elites plays a different role in what can be seen as a three-stage sequence. In the first stage, the problem of development is to create frameworks of meaning that legitimate change, especially for status groups with a vested interest in the status quo. A broad ideology which links traditional symbols of authority and meaning to the idea of change and thus fuses the past with the future in the contcext of familiar cultural elements is required not only to win the support of vested interests but also to motivate and activate those middle class groups which may already be predisposed to change.

The second-stage development problem involves the translation of ideological commitments to change into social arrangements that bring together hitherto uncoordinated scarce resources, that promote cooperation and compromise, and that mobilize the population to undertake common developmental tasks. This is the stage at which many Latin American sequences falter: Key sectors of a society may be committed to change, modernization, and even revolution, but they find it impossible, even when they have political power, to get the system moving—to work committed energies and capacities into a steady, disciplined pattern of growth. The mechanisms of mobilization—pooling resources, delegating authority, and "trusting the system"—are extremely weak and in some instances almost nonexistent.

The third stage of Latin American development is full-fledged modernization, a phase in which the mobilization mechanisms have been institutionalized, and change, both social and ideological, is accepted by all major groups in society. In this third stage old forms of solidarity and integration have been shattered, and people are "on the move" in both physical and social space. The developmental problem is to establish a new level of social integration, both vertical and horizonal, that is congruent with the demands of modernization. Thus a sequence of societal development poses three major imperatives:

—shifting the locus of meaning from tradition to change;
—transforming societal acceptance of the desirability of change into actual mobilization patterns;
—developing new modes of integration to replace traditional bonds and sustain full modernization.

Though these developmental requisites are of a different order from the ones normally considered imperative for modernization—capital, industry, or the universal franchise—they call attention to the deeper social transformations that development requires.

If the foregoing model of Latin American development is accepted, the distinctive contributions of the new religious elites can be identified at each stage. The papists perform at least two critical functions during the first stage of change. First, they link traditional Catholic values with the concept of social change, thereby utilizing papal authority as expressed in the social encyclicals to legitimate the idea of change. Second, they emphasize the principle that the church does not intend to impose its conceptions of the good society on others by political means. Rather it intends to promulgate the Catholic social ideology through a lay apostolate which will link church and society and carry the new values.

The papists' contributions are particularly relevant at the first stage because it is at this point that the church is under heavy attack for its political involvements and resistance to change. By giving Catholic legitimation to social change the papists help to overcome conservative reactions. Moreover, their efforts to strengthen the internal spiritual resources of the church within a traditional hierarchical framework ready the Catholic system for the competitions to be met in a modern pluralistic society.

In their attempts to bring about social justice and to aid in other reforming groups, the pluralists assist in the mobilization required for the second stage of development. To be effective, their approach depends upon the incorporation of some of the emphases of the papists: lay responsibilitiy in the world, an ideology linking Catholic values with social change, and the noninvolvement of the church in political affairs. Within this context, the pluralists cooperate with non-Catholic groups in economic, technical, and welfare projects characterized by a maximum of lay responsibility and a minimum of church presence. The cooperative efforts, though decidedly modest in scale, hold an enormous potential for mobilizing disparate groups to undertake the tasks of social development.

With the lack of strong support for interpersonal cooperation, the vulnerability of social consensus when attained, and the absence of functional integration between levels of social structure, the pluralists' effort to bridge traditional social and functional cleavages under the aegis of an ideology which can draw upon wide consensus of a religious nature are especially valuable for mobilization purposes. They serve not only as actual centers of mobilization efforts but also to demonstrate symbolically that much social good can come out of intergroup cooperation.

The contributions of the pastors to long-range social development are more indirect than those of the papists and pluralists, but they are equally important. When the society has begun to move into the third stage of full modernization, old patterns of identity, association, and integration have been broken and new modes of integration are urgently needed to prevent social and personal disorganization. In their efforts to strengthen the internal spiritual life of the church at the grassroots level by transforming the parish church into a source of identity and basis of social integration for the individual, the pastors function as creators of small religious and social systems on the local level which answer some of the problems stemming from mobility and social isolation. The local church provides a stable source of social identity, religious expression, and cultural anchorage, as well as mediating between the individual and society. Because the church is omnipresent in an otherwise constantly changing society, these pastoral trends provide for the critical modicum of integration needed at the grassroots level to overcome individual and communal disorientations which might otherwise erupt in social conflict.

An overall picture of the role of the three new elites can be obtained by linking the model of Latin American development, the levels of the sociocultural system, and the activities required at each point in time.

Examples of the actual operation of this model can be seen in Colombia, Argentina, and Chile. Despite its recent land reforms, its coalition government, and its internationally oriented economy, Colombia is generally considered an extremely traditional country. Roman Catholicism is the official religion, and the church controls most of the country's educational system. The clergy walk the streets with a casualness that can only come from a secure position in society. Colombia is not only a clerical country, it is also a country that is not yet fully committed to the necessity for social change. Many power groups not only resist the idea of change but manage to obstruct even minor social reforms.

The most visible new elites in the Colombian church are

ROLE OF NEW ELITES—CHRONOLOGICAL DEVELOPMENT

Levels of the Sociocultural System	Legitimating Change	Mobilizing Resources	Reintegrating Society
Culture	PAPISTS		
Intergroup		PLURALISTS	
Person-Group			PASTORS

the pluralists: there is a solid core of pluralists engaged in activities bearing directly on the solution of social problems, but there is also a growing, volatile group of pluralists who want to make a direct frontal attack on changing the social order, through revolution if necessary. This latter group has become highly visible recently, especially through the activities of a recently killed priest who had renounced his priesthood, openly criticized the Cardinal, joined the mountain guerillas, and published a manifesto for social revolution. Like many of the other radical pluralists, he claimed that true Christianity was not possible under Colombia's present social and political conditions.

These radical pluralists appear to be a concrete manifestation of a "missed stage" in the evolution of the church. Because the crucial contribution of the papists has not been made, the new elites are turning directly to secular change without the support of Catholic social ideology which legitimates development and moderniza- tion. This is a tragic situation for both the church and Colombian society. For the traditional hierarchy to legitimate the more radical pluralist strategies at this time would be too destructive of their own authority; at the same time, the conservative secular groups are not prepared to confront the problems pointed up and attacked by the pluralist priests and laity. If both of these tradition-oriented sectors had been prepared for these developments by contact with a modern Catholic ideology, the pluralists might have won their support in building an effective social action movement. Theoretically, if the more radical pluralists were to retrench and consentrate their energies on the development of such an ideology, the stabilization and reintegration of the church could be accomplished and the context set for the pluralists to move out into direct social action again.

Argentina faces a different set of developmental problems. Urbanization and technology, bursts of vigorous economic growth, and a commitment to change by major societal groups are basic features of the society; much of the groundwork for complete modernization already exists. However, the pattern of development is not steady because there are only weak bases for long-range mobilization. Factionalism, nonproductive competition, and distrust deplete energies and resources. During the Peronist era, skilled workers achieved levels of economic gratification that were unrealistic in the economic long run, and these groups are now unwilling to relinquish their gains for the national good. Intergroup tensions are especially strong in the metropolitan area of Buenos Aires, where both Protestants and Jews constitute sizable minority groups. In short, Argentina's central developmental problem is that of mobilization, drawing the already commitments to change into a working frameowrk of cooperative effort. The resources are available, but they remain uncombined and unaligned at strategic institutional junctures.

In this period of transition, the Argentinian church is a curious mixture of the traditional and the progressive. The leadership tends to be traditional without being reactionary, perhaps because all hierarchical vacancies must be filled with the approval of the government. Many of the top positions are filled by the sons and grandsons of Italian immigrants, a circumstance which has produced a combination of Italian Catholic orientations and a nationally focused church, and Catholic Action groups are relatively strong, especially among students and some of the middle-class groups. Thus, the church actually stands midway between papist and pluralist elite developments. Catholicism and the idea of change have been fused at numerous points throughout the system, but very little in the way of action-oriented cooperation has been undertaken. Part of the pluralistic deficiency is due to divisions within the hierarchy and factionalism among lay groups. There is no doubt but that a greater participation in intergroup and interfaith action projects, such as the pioneering ventures in the Buenos Aires area, by church elites would have a major symbolic effect on breaking other forms of deadlock. The new Catholic elites of the pluralist type thus appear to be the key to reinforcing the society's mobilization process.

The Chilean situation is quite different in that Chile appears to be approaching full modernization. The country has experienced chronic economic problems, exasperating political battles, and an internal migration which has created severe problems of urbanization without full industrialization. Yet political development over the past 50 years has been quite steady, and social welfare programs have been institutionalized on a nationwide basis. A major program is currently in the first stages of implementation, as are recent agreements to nationalize foreign-owned mining operations. In short, Chile seems to be "on-the-way."

The Chilean church is often and approximately called "the most progressive Catholic system in Latin America." The key positions in the hierarchy are occupied by liberals, and the church has developed and legitimated a powerful social ideology for a "Christian revolution." In Chilean Catholicism, as in the society at large, the idea of social change is fully institutionalized in a variety of programs: technical training for the *campesinos* (peasants), distribution of church lands to underprivileged groups, and credit and productive cooperatives in some of the *callampas* (urban slums). In these pluralist activities, the church has developed strong linkages with private and governmental units, but the church itself is not involved in politics. Catholic loyalties are channeled through the recently victorious Christian-Democratic party for political purposes. In short, the Chilean Catholic elites have shown a rare ability to legitimate social change in terms of symbols that bridge past and present and to develop and support cooperative undertakings for the social good.

However, it would be a mistake to conclude that continued development is assured. There is a distinct possibility that the new elites may become so enamored of their success that they will succumb to the temptation of moving directly into politics, a development which might prove disastrous for both the church and the country. On the other hand, while it has a strong, liberalized hierarchy, the Chilean church does not have deep religious anchorages among the people; the local church is not a central focus of spiritual or social activity, and the Protestant Pentecostal groups have made solid inroads into traditionally Catholic populations. The most positive line of development for the Chilean church would thus be to encourage the pastoral elites in their strategies in order to reinforce Catholic loyalties and build up the local church as a new basis of religious and social solidarity.

The three cases of Colombia, Argentine, and Chile suggest that Catholic developments are not merely correlative with societal developments, but actually play a causal role: Both Colombia and Argentina are being held back by the hesitancy and underdevelopment of the Catholic system, while Chile progresses on the basis of a change-oriented Catholic outlook.

These optimistic appraisals of the developmental potential of the new Catholic elites for Latin America imply three things. First, religious elites may play a role in the process of total societal change, particularly at the strategic levels of symbolizing intergroup solidarity, legitimating institutional reforms, and drawing marginal peoples into values and relationships that form the basis of a modern society. Ever since the enunciation of the Weber thesis, centering on the indirect consequences of religiously based motives for economic development, sociologists have been energetically searching other religions to see if parallels to the Protestant ethic are present. Hinduism, Buddhism, and Islam have all been brought under scrutiny. If evidence for something like the Protestant ethic is not found, the whole topic of religion's relevance to institutional change is dropped. Roman Catholicism, with its sacramentalism, its hierarchical system of authority, and its corporatist conceptions of society is, of course, automatically taken to be the complete antithesis to social change. But the Weber thesis has perhaps blinded us to the important theoretical point that religions may have various positive consequences in spheres of life other than the economic and through mechanisms other than the unconscious strivings of believers to transform the world in order to build the Kingdom of God.

In giving a major role to the social effects of the Catholic religious factor, it must be remembered that the importance of Catholicism is not adequately indexed by measures of church attendance or the people's conformity to the church's official moral rules. It derives more from the fact that politics, production, and personal meanings are all indirectly imbued with Catholicism and its redemptive weltanschauung. In the midst of misery, confusion, strife, and dissillusionment, Latin Americans seek a convincing plan of redemption and membership in some beautiful crusade.

This Catholic culture and its corresponding Catholic psychology must also be joined by the fact that the church as an organization has some impressive sociological features: It is the only formal organization that spans the four and a half centuries of Spanish-American history and that transcends national boundaries. While there are individual national churches, it still remains true that the Latin American church is an entity in and of itself. It possesses a distinct identity in relation to other sectors of the international Catholic church and has formal solidarity and integration in the form of such structures as the Latin American Bishop's Council, the Latin-American Religious Confederation, and the International Federation of Institutions for Socio-Religious and Social Research. These formal structures are augmented by a multitude of durable informal relationships which have developed around common interests, from temporary alliances,and as a member of confidence structures. Finally, the church is the only organization in any given country which maintains close contact with both the people and the rulers. Not only does its vertical span encompass the whole range of social scale, but its horizontal, or functional, span takes in a wide range of ritual, educational, and social associations. In short, the church is not only historically comprehensive and internationally continuous, but it is also vertically and functionally organized to encompass or touch most of the aspects of social and societal life.

There is no intention here to build the church up into some sort of complete or unique system; the argument here is that any approach to Latin America must consider Catholicism and that any consideration of Catholicism in Latin America must deal with the church as a social system of major historical and contemporary importance. Catholic elites play central roles in the process of total societal change, particularly in symbolizing intergroup solidarity, legitimating institutional reforms, and drawing marginal groups into the relationships that form the basis of an integrated modern society.

It must be noted that the capacity of the new Catholic elites to assist in development depends on their ability to generate "spiritual" authority in the secular realm without falling into a political strategy; once the religious nature of the elites is compromised by political involvements, they lose the motivating and sanctioning halo of the "spiritual" realm and become as other interest groups.

Latin American development also depends on the continuation of the breach between the new Catholicism and the traditional order. Unless secular reformers are willing to link their forms of production, their political objectives, and their goals of social revolution with progressive Catholic elites' efforts, Latin America will continue to manifest regressive swings, political setbacks, and familiar patterns of disturbance and resistance. One cannot expect new conceptions of authority, attitudes toward performance, and norms of trust and cooperation to pervade the social order unless they are anchored in the new Catholic efforts under way. In effect, this new Catholicism is the point of leverage between Latin America's past and its future, and the new Catholic elites may prove to be the most important "transition" groups in twentieth-century Latin America.

June 1967

FURTHER READING:

Church and State in Latin America: A History of Politico-Ecclesiastical Relations by J. Lloyd Mecham (Chapel Hill, N. C.: University of North Carolina Press, revised edition, 1966).

The Church and the Latin American Revolution by Francois Houtard and Emile Pin, translation by Gilbert Barth (New York City: Sheed and Ward, 1965).

The Conflict Between Church and State in Latin America edited by Frederick B. Pike (New York City: Alfred A. Knopf, 1964).

Christianity and Revolution: The Lesson of Cuba by Leslie Dewart (New York City: Herder and Herder, 1963).

NOTES ON CONTRIBUTORS

Charles Y. Glock   "Will Ethics Be the Death of Christianity" and
"Is There an American Protestantism"

Chairman of the department of sociology at the University of California in Berkeley. With Rodney Stark he is co-author of *Religion and Society in Tension, Christian Beliefs and Anti-Semitism* and *American Piety.*

Jeffrey K. Hadden   "A Protestant Paradox—Divided They Merge"
and "The Marching Ministers"

Professor of urban studies at Tulane University. He is author of *A House Divided,* a study of the involvement of clergymen in the civil rights struggle, as well as several other books including *The Gathering Storm in the Churches.* (For more detail, see the back cover.)

C. Dale Johnson   "When Ministers Meet"

Professor of sociology at San Diego State College and chairman of the local Academic Senate. His main interest is in the sociology of religion and he has also lectured and written on problems of education.

Guenther Lewy   "The Future of the Islamic Religion"

Professor of government at the University of Massachusetts in Amherst. His current research includes a comparative study on religion and revolution. Along with other books and articles, he is author of *The Catholic Church and Nazi Germany.*

Milton Rokeach   "Paradoxes of Religious Belief"

Professor of psychology at Michigan State University. His interests include relationships between political and religious beliefs. Among his works are *The Three Christs of Ypsilanti.*

Raymond C. Rymph   "The Marching Ministers"

Assistant professor of sociology at Purdue University. A social psychologist, he has worked in the civil rights aspects of a national survey of clergymen.

165

Rodney Stark   "Will Ethics be the Death of Christianity" and "Is There an American Protestantism"

Research sociologist at the Survey Research Center at the University of California in Berkeley. With Charles Y. Glock he is co-author of *Religion and Society in Tension, Christian Beliefs and Anti-Semitism* and *American Piety*.

Richard F. Tomasson   "Religion is Irrelevant in Sweden"

Professor and chairman of the department of sociology at the University of New Mexico. His book *Sweden: Prototype of Modern Society* contains a larger and more scholarly version of his article in this book.

Ivan Vallier   "Challenge to Catholicism in Latin America"

Professor of sociology at Crown College, University of California at Santa Cruz. His current research includes a study of politics and religious ecumenism with field work in the United States, Europe and Latin America. He is author of *Catholicism, Social Control and Modernization in Latin America,* among other works.